REMINISCENCES OF A STONEMASON

REMINISCENCES OF
A STONEMASON

BY A WORKING MAN

LONDON
JOHN MURRAY, ALBEMARLE STREET, W.
1908

TO THE READER

THIS is not a literary work, but a true and faithful description of the everyday life (during practically half a century) of an everyday working man

THE AUTHOR.

1908.

CONTENTS

viii CONTENTS

REMINISCENCES OF A STONEMASON

CHAPTER I

INFANCY

My father was a tradesman, who, like many others, left his native village and came to London to seek employment.

While working in London he met my mother, who was a domestic servant, also from the country. After a brief acquaintance they were married, and my father settled down in business in my mother's native place. There they prospered until a year after I was born, when my father was carried off by an illness which also seriously affected my mother's health for the remainder of her life. Thus early did one of life's shadows fall across my path. In my third year I was placed in a Home. This name is applied now to a great variety of institutions. This particular institution became my home for the next five years, and it was within its walls that I first became conscious that I was one of the many

I

separate existences in this world, and that I must think and act for myself.

Of the Home itself, considered as a building, I can say little; the only thing I can remember is that it was a large stone erection, and had a big garden attached to it. There were also some tall trees, one being a mulberry-tree; whatever the others were I can't say. One thing I well remember, a lot of crows used to fly round these trees, in the autumn afternoons especially. I am not much of a naturalist. Perhaps the crows were there all the year round; but that is the impression left on my mind.

There was a lady, whose official title would most likely be "the matron"; but we children always spoke of her as the mistress. Whether she was single or a widow I never knew, nor can I remember her name. There would, of course, be assistants, but I have not the slightest remembrance of any of them. I know some of the elder children were picked out sometimes to teach the younger ones (I was chosen myself once, but soon dismissed). So many ladies came as visitors that they have obliterated all traces from my mind of any teachers but the mistress. This lady was of middle height, dark, rather good-looking, and inclined to be stout. The most of the time that we spent indoors was occupied in reading lessons. I never remember having heard the word "arithmetic," though I can see even now the coloured balls strung on wire just as I can see the large maps which hung on the walls of the schoolroom. I remember the word "grammar," though it conveyed no meaning to my mind.

I distinctly recollect the word "music," and looking round when some of the bigger ones, in answer to questions, spoke of keys, keynotes, and so on, in the same way that I would look round now if someone near me were to commence speaking in an unknown tongue. There were no standards and no class-rooms; the infants sat and listened while the elder ones were being taught these higher mysteries. The pace was not so hot that one lot might be put out by the presence of others. The only time when we were broken up into classes was during the reading lessons, the mistress herself always taking the highest class.

My progress in reading was simply extraordinary. As there were no standards, and as the discipline was that of a Home, not a school, I cannot give any better idea of the time I took to pass from the alphabet into the highest class than this : I left the Home when I was eight, and I had then been so long in the first class that, as I have said, I have no remembrance of any instructor other than the mistress.

About a dozen of us were placed in a semicircle round the teacher. The boy at the top of the class read a sentence aloud. If he made no blunder, the next boy read the next sentence, and so on. In this manner, by counting the boys above me and the sentences, I could prepare mine and be ready when my turn came. As I was small for my age, the other boys in the first class seemed to me to live in another world, into which I could only enter during the reading lessons.

I distinctly remember one infantile success. The word "method" had been mentioned, and the mistress asked, "Can any of you give another word for method?" I think I was about halfway down the class. None of the other boys answered; the mistress looked at me, and I said, "A mode," and gained the top of the first reading class.

But out of doors it was quite different. My very first impressions of outdoor life (that is to say, in the playground, or in the garden, for we only occasionally took walks outside the gates) were utterly miserable.

While the other boys ran with hoops or played marbles and built little houses, and, above all, were shouting with glee, I seemed to be always alone and silent. One reason was, no parents visited me, and I had no cakes, oranges, or pennies to share with the rest. I had no one as a particular friend, and, as might be expected, the other boys were not slow in elbowing me to one side when there was a swing vacant and I tried to avail myself of it; or if I offered to take one of the iron hoops or wooden spades or balls, which were supposed to be common property, but which really belonged to those amongst us who could seize and keep them. I have found things to be pretty much the same in the great world outside the gates.

I must say that, as long as I allowed myself to

be pushed to one side if there was anything to be had, I was not molested by any of them. One or two things afforded me a little pleasure—watching the crows wheel round the trees, and studying the big wall maps while the other scholars were repeating their lessons. The voices of the children prevented me from feeling lonely, whilst the study of the maps afforded occupation to my mind.

At intervals we were taken out for walks. As the Home was on the outskirts of a rapidly growing city, we sometimes passed places where bricks were stacked in the middle of the road, and workmen could be seen coming up out of sewers or drains. To me these men were a distinct race who lived underground, and I used to try to imagine what it would be to live in those dark, gloomy dungeons. Sometimes our walk lay through a cemetery, where the calm repose and the clean, well-kept walks left anything but a sad effect on the mind.

One afternoon we had gone a good distance when something caused me to turn and look back. We were on the summit of a gentle hill, and my eye ranged over some wide green fields and hedges with a fair sprinkling of trees. Beyond the fields rose the spires and towers of the city. It was a glorious afternoon, and the sun's rays were breaking through masses of clouds of dark purple, a colour which is more often seen in the evening than in the afternoon. For the first time I felt the full beauty of Nature. I could have stood and gazed, but I had to move on with the rest.

Although the Home was in the suburbs, and although our walks were always towards the green fields, and therefore still farther from the slums of the city, yet one or two things combined to bring the darker side of life under our notice. The city was growing, the middle classes were moving further afield, and poverty was coming nearer. We saw plenty of ragged children, barefooted and bare-legged. We saw many men and women, whose woebegone appearance arrested the attention even of a child. On more than one occasion, when quietly walking, we had been obliged to get out of the way of a crowd attracted by a row.

The various birthdays of the children brought visitors to the Home. These visitors were another link between us and the outside world, and as they brought toys and confectionery, they unwittingly made us think that this world was a great deal brighter than the reality.

I have already said no parents visited me, therefore on my birthdays the mistress took me to tea in her own parlour. I remember this the more vividly because a great fat cat used to jump on my knee, and from there on to my shoulders, where he would purr and rub himself against my cheek.

On one of these occasions the mistress had a book upon the table, which I had before seen her reading very intently. I glanced at the title; it was "The Wide, Wide World." This was the first book whose name is impressed on my mind.

Bunyan's "Pilgrim's Progress" and "Sandford and Merton" are the only other books that I remember seeing at the Home. In this quiet, monotonous style the five years passed, and these are the few events which made a slight ripple in the regular, well-ordered calm which prevailed at the Home; and I now come to my departure from it, and my entrance into the great outside world.

CHAPTER II

BOYHOOD

My paternal grandparents were living in one of the northern counties, and had sent one of my father's sisters, Aunt Kate, to conduct me to the village where they lived.

Aunt Kate was in many respects a most remarkable woman, and although only thirty-eight years old when she came to take me in charge, had already been a widow twenty years. She was of middle height, rather stout, with the strength of a giant and all the soft outlines of a woman. Her face, seen in profile, appeared rather masculine, but seen full face there was nothing masculine in the glance of those bluish-grey eyes which had all the softness of a Madonna, but when roused could look down a madman.

She had little schooling, but strong common sense. Fashion in dress she set completely at defiance. Always working, she enjoyed perfect health, and I have no doubt that she would have lived to be a centenarian but for an accident which caused her death when she had well passed eighty years.

Of course, she had one or two defects, yet it was long before I could see any of them. One slight weakness was she did so much for her two children that in the end they were unfit to cope with the terrific struggles of modern life.

Such is a slight and imperfect sketch of my Aunt Kate, who soon won my entire confidence.

At the time of which I am speaking third-class fares were not universal as at present, and from motives of economy, after taking the train to London, we went by a steamboat a great part of the journey.

I shall never forget the start of the boat. We were all downstairs in the cabin. Suddenly I heard an uproar overhead—the sailors shouting, and chains clanking, and then stampedes from one side of the boat to the other. Gradually things calmed down. I ran upstairs to see what was the matter. The deck was all in confusion, but I enjoyed running about, and when I came down again Aunt Kate was making tea. She had provisions with her in the real old country style.

After we had come to the end of the steamboat journey, we again took train, finally arriving at a small town about twenty miles from Mosston, for such was the name of our final destination. Here I lost sight of my aunt for a time. I expect that, according to her vigorous country manner, she walked that twenty miles, and knowing it was rather too much for me, left me to be called for by the carrier. This was in the old-fashioned days.

Davison, the carrier, was as great an original in his way as Barkis in "David Copperfield," though his peculiarities only dawned on me gradually during my stay in Mosston. I felt too strange and new to everything around me to pay much attention to his person, and the country through which we slowly passed was so different from that which I had left that my gaze was riveted on it alone.

Instead of the soft pastoral valleys, where the hedges were so numerous that the trees in them seemed like a wood when seen from a distance, here was a bare range of hills on one hand and on the other a range of still more desolate hills covered with heather, but rendered a little more picturesque by their irregular forms and the numerous masses of rocks covered with moss which dotted their surfaces. Between these two ranges of hills the land was divided into farms, well tilled, no doubt; but the fields were so large and so uniform in shape, and offered to the eye so many stretches of ploughed land, that the general impression was one of nakedness.

The fields devoted to grass had mostly a moorland character, being half covered with gorse or whin, which last was the local name. Only close to the farmhouses were some of the fields of a smaller size and of a more fertile appearance, having evidently been cultivated many more years than the larger ones that stretched away towards the uplands.

The farm-buildings were all large and solidly

built of stone, but very few of them had any trees near them, and their great size made them appear still more desolate. Of course, I did not see all this at once, but the general impression left on my mind was as I have said.

While I was gazing on these new scenes, Davison was quietly watching for opportunities of hearing me speak (so I afterwards learnt), for the difference of dialects, rapidly dying out now, was then much more marked. This was his verdict afterwards: "Look you, he wasn't the size o' that; I could lift him out and in the cart with one hand, and he could talk like *Old Moore's Almanac.*"

Slowly as we proceeded, yet at length the steady old horse brought us to the end of our journey, and we came at last to the village of Mosston.

CHAPTER III

BOYHOOD (*continued*)

IT was dark when the cart stopped at the door. Davison took me in his arms and carried me inside, finally placing me on my feet on the stone floor of the kitchen of an old-fashioned village public-house.

I can see to-day the old-fashioned fireplace, with a pot built in on the left-hand side and a round oven on the right. The oven door let down on two little cast-iron brackets. I was at once placed on a seat by the oven, the door let down, and on this, as on a table, some bread and bacon and a mug of coffee set, and while I was enjoying this with a good appetite, my relations and a few customers were eyeing me with eager curiosity.

The kitchen, which was also the taproom, was low, a tall man almost reaching the joists of the ceiling; on these joists hung sides of bacon and hams and a few bunches of herbs. There was only one small square window to this kitchen, and as the walls were very thick, it was only in the summer-time that it was really light. In the winter evenings I have many a time seen this room lit up with only one candle and the firelight, yet nobody seemed at a loss, and only the very aged wore spectacles. This room, then, was practically the kitchen, sitting-room, taproom, bedroom, and parlour all together, for though there were other rooms, they were reserved for special occasions.

The premises, in fact, were rather oddly constructed, and require a little explanation. They were divided into two parts, the old and the new. The old part was only one story high, the new two. On the ground-floor there was no communication between the old and the new except by coming out of the back-door or the front of each and then walking a few yards till the next door was reached. But the top story of the new part could be reached (from a small room which was really a continuation of the taproom) by a narrow, awkward staircase. At the top of this staircase there were two doors, one leading into the new part, which was fitted up as two bedrooms, and the other leading into what was called the barracks, the said barracks being an attic or garret formed by the sloping sides of the tiled roof of the old part of the building. This was only lit by two glass tiles, which were set in the roof among the clay ones. The bottom part of the new premises was divided into a shop and sitting-room in the front, with the front-door between them, and a workshop and stable at the back. The whole premises opened at the back into a garden with a small field, which was really a continuation of the garden.

It was a very composite family that occupied these premises. First there was my grandfather, whose name was on the sign, and who was the tenant, though, as he was an old man at the time when I came, he left all in the hands of my Aunt Kate, who herself became the tenant when he died about eighteen months after. Then there was my grandfather's brother, a pensioned-off gentleman's servant, who boarded with them till his death, a few years after my arrival. Next came Uncle R., one of my father's brothers; he was a tailor in business for himself, and occupied the shop and two rooms in the new premises.

My grandmother, Aunt Kate, and Uncle R.'s wife made up the female part of the family. My grandmother was a little, active woman, whose one pride was to tell of her family. "Ten," she used to say—"I brought ten up to man and woman." Uncle R.'s wife was a very quiet woman, devoted to her husband.

Aunt Kate was the life and soul of the place, and was at home in everything she put her hand to, whether milking the cow, or digging in the garden, or serving the customers in the tap-room.

The village consisted of about twenty houses, built at various distances from the road, some with large gardens attached to them, some joined in a block, and others detached. A small stream crossed the road at one end of the village, and then ran parallel to the road. There were no houses on this side of the road, but a stone wall separated the road from the stream.

The most of the inhabitants were what is called in the country "old standards." These were the tradesmen. There was an auctioneer, a fine old Tory, always with his hat on one side and his left hand in his vest pocket. The blacksmith was a well-known character for miles round. He and his son seemed to be always working, and the smithy was the local House of Commons. If a pig was to be rung, or a hive of bees was going to cast, or, best of all, if a chimney was on fire, he was promptly on the spot, able and willing to do everything only let him have all his own way.

The village carpenter and joiner was another well-known man in the district. He made most of the furniture for those who got married, and what he made could be depended on. He had a sawpit, and the village boys used to like to watch him and his apprentice sawing trees up by hand. The lad was always in the pit, with a veil over his face to keep the sawdust from falling into his eyes. Davison Brothers, the carriers, lived at the top of the village; they were both single, and their sister kept house for them. Saturday and Sunday they wore the same clothes, and though they had the name of being very wealthy, no one would have thought it to look at them.

The rest of the population were mostly farm hands, or "hinds," as they were called. At the time when I first knew Mosston there was a lot of draining going on, and this was mostly done by Irishmen working on piece.

These Irishmen made things lively in the village. They spent their money freely, and were good customers at the public-house. I got to know them nearly all, for they found that I could write a good round, legible hand, and, above all, never stuck at the spelling of the Irish names. I was always in request to write letters. I got a penny for each letter, which penny my aunt always made me put in a box, which was called a "thrip-box."

The first two years of my stay in Mosston were very prosperous years for the village. The Crimean War started, flour was dear, and the farmers grew a lot of corn and employed a lot of extra hands. The drainers working on piece could leave off when they liked, and the one village street was lively with men playing quoits for beer by the roadside.

The children used to sit on the top of the stone wall that bordered the road, and watch the players. When the harvest came, a lot more Irish crossed over, and made a stir for about three weeks. During the harvest it sometimes happened that a row would start among these harvesters. I remember one time when all the villagers had their doors and windows fastened, and the village street was taken up with two opposite parties of Irish armed with sickles. But there was very little damage done, and nobody ever knew what the row was about, or how the two sides were pacified.

There was one striking feature about these Irish that everybody remarked; it was this: when they got paid on the Saturday, they first of all loaded themselves up with provisions for the coming week, the women carrying them in clean white bags. Then they all adjourned to the public-house and drank the remainder of the money. When they began to get elevated they always started to talk in their own native tongue, and I noticed that it was generally the women who commenced.

When the harvest was over, the bulk of them went back to Ireland, but the drainers worked on through the winter. The one striking difference that I notice when I look back on those days is the change in the physique of the men. Then wrestling and putting the stone were looked upon as nice little recreations, even after a hard day's work. Now wrestling is practically extinct, and cycling is about the only pastime that demands any exertion.

Another sport that gave the villagers both excitement and profit was what they called salmon-catching. I say what *they* called because I am aware that experts deny that the fish thus caught were salmon. Be that as it may, at the time of which I write they got no other name, and an exciting sport it was. The men went in gangs with their faces blacked, and, holding lights over the water, they were enabled to spear the fish by scores, and sometimes by hundreds. There was one local stream where the fish at certain times were so thickly packed that they could be caught by cartloads—that is, if these gangs were not stopped by the watchers. As these runs of fish took place during the winter, they filled up what would have been otherwise a dull period in the lives of the natives.

CHAPTER IV

SCHOOL DAYS

IT was in my third year's experience of village life in Mosston that I began to realize the force of that lusty and vigorous, though somewhat animal, existence by which it was marked.

Arriving in the spring, I at first felt the air rather rude and chilly. My grandmother would not let me go to the village school till winter ; by this means I had time to run about and get myself hardened a little. Besides, in Mosston the school in the summer was comparatively deserted, whilst in the winter it was filled, even young men and women (after working all the summer) attending.

During this summer my grandmother had her hands full. Once I was fished out of the brook. I had been lying on the bank sucking up the water through a straw ; and once I had no more sense than to interfere with the bees in the garden. In the evenings I sat and read. There were heaps of *London Journals, Reynolds' Miscellanies, Family Heralds*, etc., besides a good stock of more solid reading.

I was soon noticed by some of the men who came regularly, and saw me always reading.

Grandmother took a pride in my answers to their questions, and was delighted at the praise I won from the Irish for writing their letters. When I did go to school I found that I could read as well as the biggest scholars; and though my hand-writing was rather uneven, yet there was no doubt about my spelling when dictation was given. There was only one teacher, a mistress; no standards, and no discipline.

When play time came I was almost like Gulliver among the Brobdingnagians. Luckily, I soon struck up a bargain with some of the bigger ones who were puzzled with arithmetic, especially the rule of three, as proportion was named at the school. This bargain took the form of an alliance: I helped them inside, they helped me outside. As there was no discipline, no remark was made when a boy would bring his slate with a question that he found difficult. The religious question was solved in a delightfully simple manner. Every Wednesday the Roman Catholic children were put through their catechism, the rest of the school-children never taking any notice. The mistress was a Roman Catholic, and there-fore was at home with the questions.

My first winter at school slipped quickly past, and the next summer I went very little, spending most of my time playing, and watching the men playing quoits. This was good policy on the part of my grandparents, and laid the foundation of that vigorous health which I have always enjoyed. Meanwhile (unnoticed by me for a long time) a change was working itself out in my new home. I have said that Uncle R. occupied the shop and rooms on the ground-floor of the new part of the premises, carrying on a business as a tailor and draper.

Uncle was a man six feet high and broad in proportion, very humorous without being witty, better cut out for being a landlord than a tailor; and as he could step from his workshop into the garden, and then, after walking about five yards, step into the taproom by the back-door, it happened that he was often to be found enjoying himself with some of the customers. He could tell a good tale, and always had a laugh ready if anyone else told one.

As Aunt Kate was here and there and always busy, and as grandfather was old and feeble, uncle came gradually to be almost always either with the customers or working in the garden and the field. There was a quoit pitch in the field, just at the back of the garden, and this was another attraction. I, as a child, used to notice him walking from one pin to the other. He had a pair of old shoes, with the heels cut clean out, so that he could kick them off when he wanted to jump on his tailor's seat, and when he was playing he generally had a skein of tailor's drab thread round his neck ready for use when required. I have said that his wife was a very quiet woman, devoted to her husband.

Things went on like this till uncle gave up his trade, and left the district, finally taking a public-house himself. My grandfather died a short time before this happened, and Aunt Kate's son, whose apprenticeship to the tailoring had expired, took over uncle's business, and together with his sister, who had learnt dressmaking, occupied the shop and two rooms.

From this time Aunt Kate's name appeared on the public-house sign, and she reigned supreme over the household. Her son William and her daughter Mary were both patterns of industry, and as Aunt Kate herself did all the cooking and cleaning, besides bustling about in the evening when the taproom used to be filled, she laid the foundations of what turned out to be a considerable fortune—for the country, that is to say.

For three years and a half there was one steady tide of prosperity. Cousin William employed one and then two journeymen, his sister was fully employed at her business, and the village postmistress leaving for America, aunt secured the post-office for her daughter. The duties were not onerous, but the post brought other customers, and Aunt Kate was now in her glory. She had the strength of a giant, and never a day's illness.

At the end of three years and a half a cloud appeared on the horizon. But before I deal with this, I must relate an incident which took place before Uncle R.'s departure—in fact, he and I were the two principals engaged. I would be about nine and a half years old when it happened.

Uncle had cut some grass on a piece of waste ground about half a mile off. The nearest farmer had promised him the loan of an old horse to cart this grass home. We had a cart, so uncle had gone to the farmer and brought a set of harness himself, as he knew that I didn't know what constituted a set. It was early in the afternoon, and uncle, who was rather off-handed, said to me, "Here, take this bridle, and go to such a field. There is an old horse there; he's as quiet as a lamb. Put the bridle on him, and bring him here." Now, I didn't like this job. I was very little, and not used to horses. Had grandmother been up (she used to go to bed in the afternoon), she would not have let me go.

So I set off with sundry misgivings, reached the field, and found the old horse. He was quieter than any lamb. No lamb would have stood so patiently while I tried to put the bridle on his head, but could not—in fact, I was far too little for the job. How long I tried I have not the slightest idea, for I was not the one to give up. I, even when I had reached the gate on my way home, went back again, determined to succeed, but I could not. At last I set off home for good.

When I reached home I saw uncle standing outside the house waiting for me. As soon as he saw me he shouted : " You d——d lazy animal, stir your pegs !" These words have burnt themselves into my memory ; and besides, they came up again. I say this because I don't pretend to remember the quarter of the wordy war which ensued, I maintaining that I had done my best uncle abusing me for a lazy young animal. But he didn't know me.

When I look back, the thing that puzzles me to this day is that I cannot remember either Aunt Kate or grandmother saying one word, though I am certain they must have been present. All this took place outside the house in the village street. At last uncle said roughly: "Well, take that harness back again" (it was still lying at his feet).

But by this time I was in the mood in which many have found themselves when treated with flagrant injustice, and also it flashed through my mind that uncle had borrowed the harness himself. Had I gone for it I would have felt myself bound to take it back.

I said I would not.

Uncle immediately seized a rope (he had it ready to tie the grass on the cart), and started to lash me with it. I instantly threw myself on my face in the middle of the road, putting my arms so that the rope could not catch my face sideways. How long he lashed I don't know; everything seemed in a mist, nor do I know whether any of the villagers interfered; but I know that I did not take the harness back again, nor was I ever asked. The subject was never once mentioned by any of my relatives.

The only thing that I know was said by

Davison, the carrier, every time I saw him for a long time afterwards. He would stop me, and, placing a finger under my chin, say: "He would make a rare soldier; he never flinched." Years afterwards he met my wife in a train, and said the same thing.

CHAPTER V

CHANGES

THREE years and a half elapsed—it was about my thirteenth birthday—when the cloud, as I have said, appeared on the horizon. It began like this: the local squire lived about two miles off, and his servants often had dresses made by my Cousin Mary. This and the post-office together formed a connection between our house and the hall.

A young woman came to the hall. I don't know what was her exact position, but she was not what is commonly called a servant. My Cousin William, who was then a young man of twenty-five and had a prosperous business, became engaged to this young woman, and everything seemed to point to a happy and suitable marriage, when suddenly the match was broken off.

What was the matter I don't know, and, as I have said, Aunt Kate never spoke about her affairs—at least, in my hearing. One thing is certain, the young lady acquitted my cousin of all blame, and, indeed, his subsequent conduct showed that he had deeply loved her. He paid off his journeymen, gave up his business altogether, and in the end became a soured misanthrope.

I had now, thanks to Aunt Kate's and grandmother's generous care, grown considerably, though still below the Mosston standard. I had been to school three winters; but, strange to say, never got a prize, although at the top of the school. Changes had silently worked in the village. Draining had ceased, and about this time the first reaping-machine made its appearance in the district, just when corn was beginning to be less cultivated. Already the heartiness of the village life was decaying. Young men and women no longer came to school in the winter, and the first house in the village stood empty, to be followed slowly but surely by others.

Speaking of houses, there is one word that more than anything reminds me of the difference between now and then. I lived eight years in Mosston, and I deliberately state that I never once heard the word " rent," nor did I ever see anyone pay rent. " Farm-rent," of course, did crop up, but "house-rent" never.

One afternoon I came home from school, running and jumping into the kitchen. I looked round; everything seemed desolate. Aunt was crying; my grandmother was dead. As usual, she had gone to bed after dinner. Aunt had called her; she never answered. Thinking she was asleep, aunt came back, and after awhile called her again; no answer. Aunt looked in the bed; she was gone. I went outside and

leant against the wall.   A boy was standing by.
He said: "What is the matter?"   I told him.
He said: "You have lost a good friend."

A year passed without any marked events.
Aunt took me from the village school, and sent
me during the winter to another a mile off, which
was taught by a master, and therefore, she thought,
would be better.

But it was just on the same level as the other.
The only difference it made to me was this—the
master liked a drop, and finding himself sometimes
in the pub, he took the chance to praise what he
was kind enough to call my talents.   Poor fellow!
he was found drowned in about six inches deep of
water a few years afterwards.

I now began to get a slight name in the district
as a scholar.   Aunt said to me one day: "Was
James I. ever King of France?"   I replied, "No."
She then asked me why he was called King of
France in the preface to the Bible.   But this was
beyond me.

Another village lad and I attended a church
about two miles off.   It was not the parish church
—that was about five miles distant.   This lad
and I went regularly to the Sunday-school.   The
vicar was a kind-hearted gentleman, a bachelor,
and when he found that I really read the books
that I borrowed every week from the Sunday-
school library, he was at great pains to recommend
the best.

I had now left the village school.   I had
at last gained the head prize; but as the squire

got married that year, and the school, so to say, was under new management, the prize was very inferior to those that had been given before. Still, it was the head prize.

In bidding good-bye to my school life in Mosston, I wish to say a few words about the other boys. They were all healthy, vigorous boys; and though not one of them seemed to care about being a good scholar, they were all well able to take care of themselves in real life.

I was always inferior in size and strength to the average, but towards the last they paid me the compliment of choosing me as counsellor if any extra difficulty cropped up, or as judge between them in case of a dispute.

This, of course, was if they referred the matter to be judged, for in most cases they simply fought it out. As I never made the slightest claim to be their leader, being quite content to follow whoever was leader for the time being, I will briefly mention one or two of the circumstances which gave me this position among them.

Boys have their cliques and rival leaders as well as men. I was to the last almost a stranger in the village, never having or seeking any influence, but always ready to abide by the decision of the majority, and I had more than once shown coolness and resource in a difficulty.

One instance will suffice. There was a small mill just outside the village having a few fields attached to it, which fields afforded work for the miller and his sons when the mill was not running.

The mill stood at the bottom of a sloping field, which contained the mill-pond and was always in pasture. The whole of this field was visible from the mill, and one side of the field was bordered by a public road and a post-and-rail fence.

One day two other boys of my own age and myself climbed over this fence, and wandered about the field till we had got into such a position that we could not get back into the road without going round two sides of the mill-pond.

The old miller, who was a very crabby fellow, saw us, and sent his dog at us. We heard a shout, and, looking up, saw the miller gesticulating with his stick and hounding on the dog. My two companions were going to run for the rail fence, but I stopped them, pointing out that we would have to skirt the pond, and that the dog was sure to catch us; and even if he did not tear us with his teeth, he would be sure to hold us till the miller came with his stick.

I said: " Let us place ourselves back to back, like a three-legged stool, and back out of the field. I will place myself so that he will come to me first, and I will make a kick at him; and when he wheels round to get behind me, you will do the same thing."

It worked like a charm. The dog came straight for me, and I made a good kick at him; he tried to take me in the rear, but the other two boys did the same, with the result that he circled round us barking, whilst we slowly backed out of the field.

The miller raved and shouted, but he was too old to run uphill; and when we came to the fence the dog left us, as if he had done all that was required of him by driving us out of the field.

Once in the road, the two boys said : " Where did you learn that dodge ?" I said I had read of wild horses forming a ring so that they all faced the wolves.

CHAPTER VI

I START TO WORK

Having done with schooling, at least as far as Mosston was concerned, the question was what employment I should follow. This question I soon found was settled, though I can't say how or when; but I have the idea that my Cousin William had the principal share in making the arrangement.

All I know is that I started on the nearest farm, along with some women, one or two boys, and some girls. The work was hideously monotonous, especially the first month. We had to get our breakfast and be in the fields by six. There was no regular time for lunch, but we got some bread and cold tea about ten o'clock. We had an hour for dinner, between twelve and one, then worked till six.

Fancy pulling couch-grass or wickens (this was the local name) by the hand out of the ground into an apron, and then casting them into a heap to be burned! This was our work for a month.

After that we had a little more variety, spreading manure in the turnip-drills, hoeing and thinning the turnips, and hoeing the potatoes, till the hay season.

This was rather a lively time, and soon after came the harvest, a still more lively time. I enjoyed the harvest, though I had to work hard, for there was a little excitement. I don't know what the field gang did after the harvest, for as soon as the last field of corn had been stacked the farmer told me that he had no further need of my services.

I felt rather nonplussed, for I expected to be employed till November 12, but my aunt seemed to be satisfied ; and as I had had no say in commencing, I had no say in leaving.

This was my first and last spell at farm work. In taking leave of it, I can only say that if the average farmer is as greedy as the one I worked for, they are to be pitied.

Some days after I had left this farmer I fell in with the miller—not the old man who had sent his dog after me, but his eldest son. He asked why I was walking about, and I told him. He said that the next spring a lad that was in his employ was going away, and that I could have his place to live at the mill and drive a horse and cart, and fill up my time on the mill farm, and he would pay me six shillings a week and my board.

As I knew that there would be no work during the winter on any of the farms, I jumped at the offer, for this was to be all the year round, and I now saw an opening out of the position of dependence on others, which was beginning to gall me, although it was through no fault of mine that I was thus placed.

I went home in high glee, thinking my aunt would be as pleased as myself at this liberal offer. To my astonishment she refused point blank to let me engage myself, and as the miller would not hire me without her consent, I was once more without any prospect of earning my own living.

As she would give me no reason for refusing, I came to the conclusion that her son William was at the bottom of it; this at least would account for refusing to give any reasons. As I have said, he was rapidly becoming a misanthrope. To do him justice, he fought against it; but he had given up his trade, and he was too proud to take it up again when he found out the evil effects of idleness.

He even went for three months to a school, with a view to entering the Civil Service, for he was still some months short of being twenty-eight, which was then the age limit of entrance. But this came to nothing, and my aunt seemed perfectly satisfied to see him under her roof, saying there was plenty to keep him, and no need for him to bother himself about any work.

How it was that with her strong common sense she did not see that degeneration would be the inevitable result I can't understand, and can only record the facts as they transpired. She told me that she wanted me to be a schoolmaster, and that there was an opening for me as a pupil-teacher at the National School in Westwick, the same small town from which I had come with Davison, the carrier. I had no idea of becoming a schoolmaster, but as this would take me away from Cousin William's sneers, I said that I would give it a trial, mentally resolving that in the spring, if I did not like it, I would run away to some distant place and work for myself, for I was now beginning to feel strong enough for anything.

I pass over the journey to Westwick, and my interview with the master of the school. It was settled between my aunt and himself that I should come as a scholar for a few weeks, previous to being finally engaged as a pupil-teacher. What was the scale of payment I cannot say, for I never got that far. The interview took place on a Saturday forenoon, there being, as we used to say, no school on the Saturdays. After arranging about my lodgings, aunt went home in the afternoon with Davison, and I was left to my own resources.

Westwick was indeed a small town, but it had a town hall, and a market-place, with a sort of market every Saturday, to which market my old friend Davison came from Mosston, so that I was still in touch with my aunt's household.

But now for the first time I had a lot of liberty, and I was going to pit myself, a country school-boy, against what I thought would be the scholars of Westwick. I say " what I thought," because, boy-like, I had no idea of the low level of education that could exist in a school with the proud title of " National." Westwick, let me say, was rather famed for schools, and justly so, but the National—well, we shall see.

On the Monday morning I was in the school-yard in good time, with my threepence in my hand. I found a lot of boys busy playing marbles, and shouting as only schoolboys can shout. I could hear the remark, " From the country"; this was good, Westwick being little more than a village. But remarks were cut short; the town clock commenced to strike nine, a side-door opened, the master blew a whistle, and we all filed in, saluting the master in passing.

I deposited the threepence on the master's desk, and took my place in the first class. The staff consisted of the master, two assistants, and one pupil-teacher. We sang something, I don't know what—I was looking all round the school —then the books were given out, and the master taking the first class, we began to read.

As soon as two or three sentences had been read I was satisfied—in fact, the general level of the first class was far below that of Mosston. This was my first disillusion; before the day was over I experienced another. The second master or the first assistant (I don't know his exact position) took the first class in the after-noon for dictation.

Now, dictation is a useful exercise, and a capital test of the pupil's intelligence; for besides spelling—well, there is room for initiative in punctuation.

Accordingly, I laid myself out for once to do my best. I had a sharp slate pencil and a clean slate, and at that time affected a rather small handwriting. When the teacher had finished reading the exercise, he took the slates from the boys, and pointed out any errors in spelling or slovenly writing: but he never offered to take mine, and as this was my first day, I patiently waited my turn.

From what I afterwards saw of this man I don't think he meant looking at my slate, but two of the boys in the class who had already had theirs examined took my slate and looked it over, and then took it up to the teacher, saying, "What do you think of that?" An unpleasant shade came over his face, and he said pettishly, "Very good, but you want spectacles to read it."

This was the first of a series of incidents that occurred at the school while I was there, and though in relating them I may appear to be boastful, they actually happened, and are recorded in order to show why I left the school and followed my own course.

Map-drawing was an exercise that we had never had at Mosston, but having been given the task to draw a map of Scotland as home-work, on bringing it the same man said that I had laid my paper over a map, and thus traced mine. I contented myself with simply denying it, but I had no parents to take up the cudgels for me.

The Vicar of Westwick used often to come in the afternoon and take the first class. He always wore a small black skull cap when doing so.

One afternoon, when he had been asking questions on the geography of Europe, and the leading events that were taking place in each country at that time, I gave him some answers after looking round the class and assuring myself first that no other boy was going to answer. He thereupon remarked that if any question the least different from the ordinary routine was asked, I was the only one that could give a reply. This was gall and wormwood to the second master, who had a cousin in the same class. This cousin lived with him, and was destined for the teaching profession.

One more incident, and this time the master himself was involved. How it came about I don't know, but the conversation in the class fell upon Australia and the kangaroo. I said that there was a small animal in the north of Africa which had short fore-legs and long hind ones, thus resembling the kangaroo. Asked the name of this animal, I replied immediately, "The jerboa." I was at once greeted with derisive laughter, the whole of the teaching staff maintaining that no such animal existed.

As the book from which I had got my information was at Mosston, and I had no one to back me up, there was nothing for it but silence, after stating that I was sorry I could not show my authority.

However, inwardly resolving that, for the

remainder of my stay, I would give them all a reminder of their conduct, I began the very next morning to put my plans into action.

I have already said that Westwick had a town hall, and that the master blew his whistle at the first stroke of nine by the town clock. Now, Westwick being such a small town, if I arrived at the school and stood outside of the door of the schoolyard, the sound of the clock was sure to reach me, no matter which way the wind blew. There were no cheap watches in those days.

My idea was to wait till the last stroke of nine had died away, and then enter the school. By doing this I would not be late enough to incur punishment, but would lose my place in the class and have to go to the bottom.

Then it was my turn to score, as they say now, and I had the satisfaction of walking up to the top as soon as any difficult sentence was reached.

After this had happened a few times, the master made some remark, which has escaped my memory, but he never seemed to see that my coming late was deliberately done. Having thus shown that I could simply play with the lessons given in the first class, I resolved to confine myself to answering only when I was directly asked.

I gladly leave this part of my school experience, and trust that I have given good reasons for refusing to become a pupil-teacher. I stated all these reasons to the master when I left, and took the opportunity of thanking him for the fair treatment that I had had from himself.

CHAPTER VII

I LEAVE WESTWICK

OUTSIDE of the school-gates I, of course, was living quite a different life from that of Mosston. I was almost like a young man in lodgings. On the Saturdays I saw my old friend Davison, the carrier, but said nothing about my future. Westwick was an interesting little town, and I tried to explore every portion of it, choosing the Saturday afternoons for long walks round the outskirts. I have said the second master had a cousin destined for the same profession. Blake was a boy about my own age, and sat next me in the school. We became companions, and as he seemed to like my society, I was asked to come any evening and spend an hour or two with him.

This to me was rather flattering, for he was staying in the same house as the second master, and I felt sure that there must be some special reason for it, as he (the second master) had no friendship for me.

I soon saw how the land lay, and then was not quite so much flattered. Blake was not very sharp, and had to do a lot of home-work at night. This necessitated staying in the house, and as my position very much resembled his own, it was providing him with a companion and a pace-maker at the same time.

There was a good piano, Indian clubs, and chess for our amusement after the lessons were finished. I knew nothing then about music, or chess, or even the Indian clubs; but as the house had a big garden, Blake and I enjoyed ourselves at quoits.

The National School was nothing if not churchy, and the piano was practised by the assistant, so that at a pinch he could take the organ at the church or play the harmonium at the school.

Blake and I took turns in blowing the organ once a week for his organ practice. At that time when the organ was playing I was just conscious of a confused mass of sound, and used to be glad when it was over. But it was a novelty to me, walking to the church and opening the gates and doors with keys without having to ask permission. The church was a very old one, and the church-yard was well kept and contained many curious old tombstones.

There were two curates besides the vicar, and I was introduced to both of them; but as soon as they knew my position and prospects, they took no further notice of me than to return my salute if I met them. Poor fellows! their own position was not a very enviable one.

There was a sort of library connected with the church, which was opened for the exchange of books on the Saturday afternoons; but the books (at least, all those that I saw) were a dreary lot, forming a striking contrast to those that can be obtained from any of the municipal libraries of to-day.

Thus the weeks rolled on, and at last the time approached for me to become a pupil-teacher. My mind was fully made up, and I had no difficulty in telling the master that I was determined not to be a teacher; but I could not so easily bring myself to an explanation with my aunt, knowing that she had done her utmost for me to the best of her judgment. I therefore took a middle course, and knowing that the master would let her know by letter of my decision, I awaited the first word from her, and sure enough in a few days I received a letter from Mosston, bidding me come on the first Saturday. As the school fees (threepence per week for me in the first class) were paid every Monday morning, there were no accounts to settle, so I continued to go to the school up to the Friday afternoon, knowing that that was my last day at school, but saying nothing to any of the scholars, not even Blake, that I was leaving.

One of the world's lessons I had already learnt —namely, to say nothing about my affairs to anyone not immediately interested in them. On the Saturday I saw my old friend Davison, and gave him my few effects in a bundle, telling him he would find me at Mosston as soon as he got there. Good old Davison! it was nearly eight years since he had taken me in his cart to Mosston, and I really felt the first pang when he looked at me inquiringly, but asked no questions.

The market-place was close to the road leading to Mosston, and at first I strolled very slowly along this road till I was at the outskirts of the town, and then, quickening my pace, I walked at a good speed, for I had nearly twenty miles to go, and I was just in that frame of mind when a good walk is a luxury. I might be an insignificant unit, an atom in the mighty universe, but none the less I had left school that day, and in refusing the career of a teacher had in a small way taken as decisive a step as Cæsar did when he crossed the Rubicon.

I remember the day was fine, though rather cold, and as I walked on and at last gained the top of a hill and looked down into the valley and saw Mosston, the fierce energy with which I had set out began to die away and be succeeded by a calm slightly tinged with melancholy.

The future had no cloud to cause this melancholy; on the contrary, I looked forward to carving out my own career with confidence. Had I not youth and health ? No, it was the present. Something told me I was soon to leave Mosston ; and besides, in an hour's time I would be face to face with the explanation due to my aunt.

I found them all unchanged, and my Cousin William in a rather more cheerful mood than ordinary. He had made up his mind to go to London and take a situation as a tailor's cutter, though I only knew this a few days after my return.

I took the first opportunity to explain my position to my aunt, and was rather surprised to see how quietly she heard me out; but I was too young then to analyze character. I now know that though she was firmness itself, she would not argue with anyone, but, as she herself expressed it, would set her foot down, and if she could not enforce her will would not express it at all. But she could not force me to become a teacher, and therefore she would not reason with me, but simply asked what I intended to do. I said I would hire myself at the March hirings, which were to take place in a few days. But as it turned out, I never went to the hirings, for in a day or two a letter came from one of my mother's brothers offering me a situation. My aunt had, unknown to me, been writing to him, for she had made a resolution that, if possible, I should not be a farm servant. Accordingly, Cousin William and I left Mosston together, and went to London, where I parted company with him, he staying in London while I went on to my uncle's residence.

I may just mention here that my cousin paid a lot of money to a firm for what is called finishing lessons in cutting, and at the end of these lessons the firm procured him a situation as cutter with a tailoring firm in one of the large provincial towns (since made a city). He had not been there long when he wrote home that his employer seemed to be trying to find fault with him. This was enough for my aunt. She at once replied, telling him to come home; there was no need for him to work for anyone.

Cousin William went home, and never sought any other employment. We shall meet him again in the course of this history; meanwhile behold me in the train alone, fairly launched into the world to earn my living by my work, and with a capital of about ten shillings. I must say that the situation in which I found myself was rather interesting. The train was speeding through the southern counties of England, and every time we emerged from the cuttings I was struck with the different aspect of the country, and the people who were working in the fields. These, instead of being clad in moleskin or corduroy, all wore smocks, and those engaged in ploughing took my attention at the very first.

Instead of two horses abreast, and one man at the plough, as in the North, there would often be three, one in front of the other, and a boy in a smock frock and a long whip would guide the horses, while a man held the plough. I have never in my life seen a ploughman in the North use a whip, though they sometimes jerk the reins so as to give a horse a slight blow.

The carts, too, were of quite a different build, and whilst in the North it was, and is, quite common for one man to have charge of two carts, the horse in the second cart being tied with a halter to the first cart, no man here seemed to

have charge of more than one. The low white-
washed cottages, with their thatched roofs that
undulated in all sorts of graceful curves, were in
striking contrast to the solid stone houses, with
ashlar fronts and slated roofs, that I had just left.

But the ditches between the fields, sometimes
lined with willows, and always appearing to be
stagnant, began to attract my gaze. No more of
the flashing trout streams, with their heaps of
gravel and well-rounded pebbles, were to be
seen. If there were any rivers, they could only
be traced by the irregular contour of their banks,
instead of the straight lines of the ditches. No
stretches of clear water reflected the rays of the
sun, but now and then I caught a glimpse of a
canal, and saw one of the long narrow boats like
snakes being towed by a sleepy old horse.

After a while the novelty of the scenes failed
to prevent my thoughts from dwelling on my
position, and I began to wish I was at the end of
the journey; not that it was tiresome, but I
wished to see what was before me, and to end
the state of suspense into which I was gradually
sinking.

At length the green fields gave place to houses;
the train gave a few alarming bumps as we
passed through a wilderness of rails, with
solitary trucks here and there, as if stranded;
one loud whistle was followed by another, and
another, the train slowed down, and then stopped
under a huge arch of iron and glass.

We had arrived at the terminus of the line by

which I had travelled, and although, by changing trains and taking a fresh ticket, it was possible to proceed on another line to my destination, business considerations combined to render it more expedient for me to go by road the rest of the journey. My uncle was waiting on the platform, and afterwards said he would have known me at once, from the family resemblance, even if he had not been expecting me. After a few remarks on the journey, we proceeded to the inn, where he had a horse and trap waiting.

The city which formed the terminus of the principal line by which I had come was the city from which he drew all his supplies, and as third-class tickets were not then issued on all trains, it was cheaper to come in with a horse and trap, which, besides conveying us two, could carry some merchandise as well.

Accordingly, we drove through a fertile country about twelve miles till we came to the village where my uncle had lived for about thirty years, and which was destined to be my home for about four years and three months.

CHAPTER VIII

LIFE AT FARNHAM

FARNHAM was a long, straggling village, bisected by a railway, which crossed the one street at right angles. Like some other villages that have never been laid out in regular streets, and yet have increased in population, it would have become too long and scattered if the original plan of building by the roadside had been carried out, so it contained one or two squares so-called, one side of these squares being formed by the main road.

It had a large church, with an open space between the churchyard and the main road, which formed the village street. This made a village green, and, if I remember correctly, the old village stocks were kept in this churchyard, the place where they formerly stood on the green being marked by a stone.

Besides the church, there were two dissenting congregations, one of which belonged to the Methodists, and the other was a sort of Independent congregation, whose exact name I never knew, and I only mention it here to show how strong the dissenters were in this locality.

There were also some Quakers, or Friends, but they had no place of worship in the village.

I was not long in finding out that both in the village and within a radius of ten miles almost all the tradesmen were dissenters, and that the exceptions to this rule were mostly butchers and innkeepers.

Why this should be the case, seeing that the Churchmen were equally intelligent, and on an average better endowed with capital, I don't pretend to know—I simply state the fact; and I have found the same state of things all through life.

My uncle was a Methodist, and one of his sons was a local preacher among them. His business was that of a wholesale and retail grocer, but he dealt largely in cheese and bacon—in fact, nowadays his business would be conducted by a limited company, and called by the name of " The Wholesale Supply Stores," or "The Direct Supply Company," or any other of the indefinite and high-sounding names that are over the shops of to-day.

But the Limited Liability Act, which has crushed out so many private tradesmen, was only coming into operation about the time I left Farnham.

After I had been round a few times among his various customers, in company with himself or my cousin, I was sent out by myself. We had three horses and a pony, and I never drove the same animal on two consecutive journeys; but although I could not be a horsey man even if I tried, I soon came to the conclusion that a pony will do more work than a horse.

Fifteen miles was about the limit of the radius of the district covered by the business, but, of course, not in the direction of the city.

The civil war in the United States, which broke out soon after my arrival in Farnham, brought a great increase to the business. Whether my uncle's dictum — that the States were pushing their produce over here to help pay for the war—was true or not I leave others to decide ; but the fact is, we suddenly almost doubled the turnover by selling American bacon, cheese, and flour. I remember that a lot of people said at first that the bread soon turned dry, though this complaint soon died out, but there was a strong prejudice for a long time against the American cheese and bacon. But cheapness and credit combined enabled us to dispose of an enormous quantity for a long time, till others overcame their dislike of American produce, and entered into competition.

Even then my uncle, in virtue of having got the start, reaped the benefit of his foresight, and found himself obliged to enlarge his premises considerably.

For about two years I enjoyed my occupation. Driving through the country even on business is an exciting and lively way of passing the time compared with being pent up indoors, besides being incomparably more healthy. After the horses and I had got fairly used to each other, I could travel for miles and read a book without any inconvenience.

There was not a great deal of traffic on the roads, and there were no cycles in those days. One of the horses had a nasty habit of shying, especially at dusk, but he was always sure on his feet ; still, as the roads were rather narrow in some places, and bordered with deep ditches, the reading was left off whenever I had this special animal.

The pony was always my favourite. He was as quiet as a lamb, and though inclined to take it easy when going out with a load, he knew when his nose was turned homewards and the cart empty. Then he would lay himself out, and I could read a book without ever having any misgivings, even where the roads were narrowest and the ditches deepest.

Horses are no more perfect than human beings, and the pony, with all his good qualities, had one slight fault, which, if he could have spoken, he might have excused on the score of obedience. If any person was standing at the side of the road, especially if they had the appearance of wishing to hail the driver, he would stop dead short if he could.

Now, on the level or going uphill this was not much, but if we were going down a bank the shafts would bend till I wondered they did not break. After one or two experiences of this nature, I used to be on my guard if I saw anyone standing near the roadside.

Most of the shops that we supplied were

4—2

kept by people who had to struggle for a living, but, to their credit be it said, we had next to no bad debts. My uncle never pushed his goods upon them, and not only was he very patient in cases where we had to wait for the money, but several of his customers acknowledged that his advice had been of very great service to them.

Of course, there were some who, in spite of all their efforts, could not go on ; but I am not going to dwell for one instant on any one of these cases, although feeling almost compelled to write down one peculiar incident that happened, but whether it was caused by poverty or family trouble I don't know.

We had supplied a small shop with goods for some time, and I had only exchanged a few business remarks with the person (a quiet, middle-aged woman) who kept it. One day I had transacted some little business in the shop, and was just going out of the door, when she asked me if I knew what would kill a mouse. I was dumb for a bit; of course I knew fifty ways, but I looked at her as much as to say, "Are you having a bit of fun ?" The first glance was sufficient; no fun was intended.

Seeing me still hesitate, she said that she had a mouse, and had been trying to kill it, but could not. "Look, here it is ;" and I followed her behind the counter.

There was a jar—I think it was an empty jam-jar—and lifting a small plate, she showed me a mouse inside. She repeated that she had tried to kill it and could not. I don't know what I said; most likely I would suggest drowning it by sinking the jar in a pail of water. I say "most likely," for when she went on to say that she had tried poison and failed, a thought flashed through my mind. I glanced at the scantily stocked room, and once more at the woman's face; I felt that I was in the presence of Something and left as quickly as possible consistent with politeness.

I kept the horrible suspicion to myself. I was only seventeen, and from infancy had known no parent to confide in; but when in a few days' time word came that the woman had poisoned herself, I gladly eased my mind by relating what I had seen, and the thought that I was afraid to utter. My uncle said I was quite right in saying nothing when there was only surmise to work on, and the matter was never referred to again.

Life in the household meantime was of the most regular and well-ordered character. Both father and son were assiduous in their attendance at the Methodist Chapel, and the son, being a local preacher, often conducted a service on week-nights. The daughters were all professed Christians, never went to a ball, and would not even read a novel, unless it were by some such writer as Emma Jane Worboise.

Not one of the family, my uncle excepted, would touch intoxicating liquor, and he himself, as well as his son, eschewed tobacco in any form. The sole relaxation was attending chapel anniversaries, tea-meetings, or going to hear some popular preacher.

Of course, the house was frequented by the regular ministers, and, as there are frequent changes among them, I was brought into contact at least thrice a week with either a local preacher or one of the paid preachers. I found them neither better nor worse than those who made no profession of religion, while their conversation might be summed up in one word—shop.

As might be expected, the class of books in this household was a very restricted one, the only book that I found really interesting being the "Autobiography of Benjamin Franklin." I read and re-read this book, and shall have occasion to refer to it again.

Sometimes my cousin would read to me a sermon that he was preparing, and ask my opinion of it, but not often. Though I admired his simple, straightforward character, we were diametrically opposite in our views and opinions. When I first knew him he was twenty-four, and I sixteen, and at the very outset a trifling incident occurred that made a slight coolness between us.

It happened thus: My uncle rented a few fields about half a mile from the house. These fields served to grow hay for his horses, and in the summer, when any horse had been on a journey through the day, on its return, after it had been fed and allowed to cool down, it was turned into one of the fields at night.

Thus, when I was being shown round at the first, it was necessary to visit these fields, as my duties would require me to take one or other of them either in the morning or at night. A young man, who was an acquaintance of the family, my cousin, and myself, walked down to these fields accordingly. It was a fine evening, and we strolled about the fields enjoying the fresh air.

This companion was a bit of an athlete, a runner and jumper, though I only got to know this afterwards. He was a total stranger to me, but from what I know now of human nature, I don't think I am doing any injustice in surmising that, besides showing off his own powers, he was quite willing to have a laugh at my expense.

Anyhow, the talk was soon about jumping, and as the grass-fields were bordered with ditches, it was very natural; and even if I had had any suspicion of being taken on, as we say now, I was certain that I could jump any of the ditches that were likely to come in our way. But I had none, and my cousin was the last one to suspect anybody.

I have already stated that running and jumping were the only exercises in which I could hold my own with the Mosston boys. The stranger led the way in walking, and I soon noticed that he took the most awkward places to cross the ditches. My cousin jumped after him, and I followed last. After two or three jumps, it was evident that the stranger was showing off, but, as I did not know him, I thought it nothing but youthful exuberanee.

But the ditches in places were very wide, as the banks had fallen in, and after we had cleared one awkward spot my cousin turned to me and said: "I didn't think you could have jumped that." I was foolish enough to say that I was a pretty good jumper. One word brought on another, and at last I said: "Well, I will jump any ditch that you can jump."

The stranger said nothing, but led the way again. I think we had made only two more attempts, when we came to a place broader than any ordinary ditch; in fact, it was close to the road, and the banks were broken down by horses coming to drink. The stranger surveyed the spot, felt the bank on which he stood, to see if it was firm enough to spring from, took a run, and got safely over. My cousin followed, but though he lighted on the bank, it was close to the edge, and he fell backwards, after a desperate effort to clutch the grass.

We dragged him out dripping wet and covered with green weed. Then he turned to me and said: "Now it's your turn." But I answered: "No. I said I would jump any ditch you can jump, and have done it, and when you jump this I will jump it." We argued for a bit, and I referred to the stranger, but he said something to the effect that it lay between ourselves. My cousin was forced to admit that he had not jumped it, and we proceeded home, and the affair was soon all over the village.

CHAPTER IX

THE STRANGER

In this quiet, sedate household I passed two years, and during that time the only event that stirred the pulse of Farnham was the marriage of the Prince of Wales, now King Edward VII. The village was no way behind in joyous demonstrations, and there were races amongst the boys and young men.

In the young men's race I was second, and won a half-crown, and was very much astonished to be told four years since that, according to that, I was a professional runner. But at the end of the two years an event took place that caused a lot of excitement at the time and changed to a great extent the tone and manner of life in the leading dissenting families of the village.

The commencement was the old - standing friction between Church and Chapel. The various taunts that passed between the two parties may be summed up in these: Chapel said that in the Church the parson was everything and the people nothing. Church replied that the chapel-goers might be very pious, but they all had a strict eye on the main chance.

As I was too young to be admitted into any of the committee meetings, I don't know how it came about, but suddenly it was resolved by the dissenters to build a new day-school. It was built, and very quickly, and a young man came from some training-school to act as schoolmaster. He was quite young—I don't think more than twenty —thin, pale, intellectual-looking, very handsome, though a lot of men would have said rather too delicate and fragile (he broadened out wonderfully in the country air), and, above all, really religious. A good musician, he used to sing the tenor part from the notes, and when he stood up in the chapel to give an address his tall figure, always in black, and his pale face took the attention of everyone.

All the young ladies were full of praise and admiration, and I really think I cannot say more in his favour than this, that when I left the village, two years later, he was then as modest and unassuming as when he arrived.

The school was almost opposite my uncle's house, and of course he often called in the evening. I have said that he changed the whole tone in the leading dissenting families. This is strictly true, for before his advent the said families seemed to have only one pursuit, that of getting money, but afterwards, though this pursuit was not neglected, there was a distinct effort to acquire a little polish: the young ladies took lessons in music, and the young men paid more attention to their language in conversation.

Farnham was not the residence of any of the Methodist preachers, but whichever preacher conducted the service on a Sunday night generally officiated at a short service on the following Monday evening. But now there was a cultured young man resident in the village, whose conversation was far above the level of these reverent gentlemen even on their own subjects, and on any others, such as music, drawing, or general information, still more so.

Having a school of their own, the dissenters proceeded gradually to form a library, with the new master as librarian, and it was due to his influence that a good selection of high-class literature was purchased. The wiseacres shook their heads, of course, but he had already made himself so popular that on this subject he was allowed a free hand, more especially as any book that he chose was certain to contain nothing that they would hesitate to put into the hands of their daughters.

In the winter penny readings were organized and given in the schoolroom, some of the readers exercising a good deal of their own discretion in the choice of authors, and some of the selections contained allusions which would have been vetoed by the old fogeys; but as the said old fogeys were comfortably seated at their own firesides, no harm was done, though I remember a thrill went through the audience when a reader, a Quaker no less, set off at full swing about Miss Kilmansegg and her golden—leg.

But as far as penny readings were concerned, the event of the session was one evening when the new schoolmaster recited " The Raven," by Edgar Allan Poe. The audience all moved in their seats when he rose to his feet, and a dead silence was maintained till he finished. He recited it well, and (as far as I could judge) with just the necessary amount of passion. The young ladies present talked of nothing else for a bit, and for a short time there was a run upon the poems of Edgar Allan Poe in the library.

I have purposely dwelt upon this young man's influence in the village because, as will be seen, he was the unconscious cause of a quiet revolution in my uncle's household, and indirectly he, unknown to himself, was going to affect my position during the remainder of my stay in Farnham. Before describing this silent change, I will mention a little incident, which, while it brought him into close contact with the family, shows how he made such an impression in a very short time.

My uncle was desirous of putting up a summer-house in his garden.

These were not the days when anyone had to deposit a plan with some local authority before being allowed to proceed with such a trifle, as he must do now. Of course, there was a little exchange of views between uncle, cousin, and the stranger as to what it should be like.

Certainly designing a construction was not the forte of either uncle or cousin, and they were pleasantly surprised when the new-comer sent them a neat little sketch of an octagonal summer-house, with highly ornamental barge boards and a full-sized detail of the moulding.

As this was gratis and just flung off in the same manner as he would have written out the music of a popular hymn-tune for any of the young ladies, it might be said of him as of Cæsar—"Came, saw, conquered."

Though the stranger was a dissenter and sometimes spoke in the Methodist Chapel, yet he was not a Methodist himself, and my cousin being, as I have said, a local preacher, it often happened that the two fell into theological discussions. In these discussions the stranger had decidedly the best of it, and my cousin admitted the fact cheerfully.

But whilst admitting the fact, he attributed it to the differences in their hours of labour, saying that the stranger only worked thirty hours a week, and he himself sometimes worked that in two days. I may say *en passant* that it was quite a regular thing for me to work the same in two days.

The schoolmaster would close the school at half-past four, go to his lodgings, have tea, wash and refresh himself, and then come to where we were working and discuss with my cousin. After he had left, cousin would say to me: "If I had the same time to prepare my subjects as he has, I would be able to hold my own with him." He began to bestir himself, and to talk with me about his position and prospects, being now in his twenty-seventh year, and no stated hours, nor, what was more to the purpose, no stated wage—in fact, he had no wage at all.

There was no doubt that the business was a paying one, but that was because all the family were working, and none drawing wages. The two men employed by my uncle, of course, were paid, but not one of the family; and over the shop-door was the sign with my uncle's name, but no—"and son." Yet the son was doing most of the work.

I simply listened to my cousin—my own affairs were demanding all my attention; and although he spoke very guardedly, yet it was evident he began to feel anxious. For a long time he had had thoughts of going into the regular ministry, and now the time was approaching when he must make up his mind.

Twenty-eight at that time was, if I remember, the limit for entering into the Methodist ministry, and he was rapidly approaching the limit. But he was now conscious that he was not cut out for a minister, and his discussions on theology with the stranger had shown both to himself and to me that his education had not fitted him in the least for the profession.

Accordingly, his mind was made up to demand a share in the business, and to have his name on the sign, and either to be paid a salary commensurate with his services, or else to be credited with so much of the capital.

This was all very good and definite, but how was it to be got?

My uncle's family was as united and happy as the average one, and even if there were any bickerings about each one's portion, that did not concern me, and I will content myself with saying (before I come to my own affairs) that when I left, more than a twelvemonth after my cousin had come to this conclusion, he had not then got anything definite

But the talks with my cousin had set me thinking of my own position, my long hours, with the slightest pocket-money, and no prospect for the future. The stranger with his thirty hours a week was ever present, and I had had another object-lesson—that is the phrase nowadays.

I have said that shortly after my arrival my uncle had enlarged his premises. I did not pay much attention to the workmen employed at the time, as my own position was still quite a novelty; but when, as often happens, the first alterations to building entailed others further on, I began to compare my hours and conditions of employment with theirs.

Certainly there was a tremendous difference between nine hours and fifteen, but that was not all—they finished work at twelve on the Saturdays, and that was precisely for me the longest day.

Except for a few weeks in the middle of the winter, there was a circumstance that made these hours for me a little longer than for any of the family. It was this, when the horses came home from a journey, they were generally pretty warm, and sometimes very hot.

This meant that, after they had been fed, they had to stand long enough to cool down before they were taken down to the fields and turned out to grass. I not only had to do this when I came home from a journey, but also when my cousin came home I had to take the one he had driven. Many a time the church clock was striking ten when I was coming back from the fields.

Certainly the outdoor life was healthy, and the many changes of scene made the hours pass a little quicker. It was also true that I had been able to do a lot of reading whilst driving.

These circumstances, as I have said, made the first two years pass very pleasantly.

But time brings changes. At eighteen I began to see that, except in years, I was making no progress at all; my labour was becoming each year more valuable, but the only recompense was a miserable apology for pocket-money, and that even was not paid regularly. Still, youth and health are so elastic that I could have borne all this contentedly, but there was as usual the last straw that breaks the camel's back.

CHAPTER X

I RESOLVE TO LEAVE FARNHAM

I HAVE said that the only book in the household that really interested me was Benjamin Franklin's "Autobiography." His dogged perseverance, and his success in improving his mind, stirred my blood, and I determined to improve my own.

With all their advantages, it was quite evident that not one of the household could hold their own in conversation with the new schoolmaster; in fact, the very points in their character, and in their views of education, on which they prided themselves were their weak points—at least, in this instance. They were so wedded to business, and what they called practical views of life, that they looked upon any reading (the Bible excepted) as time wasted.

"An ounce of practice is worth a ton of theory" was my uncle's favourite saying.

The daughters all agreed that reading fiction was, if not a sin, a weakness, and, as they said, unfitted people for business.

As a local preacher my cousin read scarcely anything but Dwight's "Theology," a diffuse, wearisome book, with the result that only his transparent sincerity procured him an audience.

As might be expected, my own fondness for general reading came in for any amount of ridicule and covert sneers, but the only reply from me was, "The proof of the pudding is in the eating of it." And a proof soon came in this manner:

There were employed in the business two vehicles called, I believe, coburgs, and a pony-trap for the pony. As there were very few third-class trains at that time, the family made almost all their jaunts in one or other of these vehicles, with the result that after I had been there some time my uncle was involved in a correspondence with the Revenue authorities about carriage licences, he considering that he was overcharged to a certain extent.

At this interval of time the exact technical point at issue escapes my memory, but this at least does not. After fruitless letters on his part, he came to me one day and stated his case, and then asked me to write a letter, based on his statements, to the authorities.

This letter produced (after an interval of waiting) a reply, satisfying him in every particular.

Did I get any thanks? No; but I felt an inward gratification.

Things were different with the arrival of the new-comer, fresh from the training college. Too polite to show that he was bored, and at the same time knowing his position depended on pleasing the majority of the dissenting families, he soon saw that, whilst the daughters of the house could not follow his conversation, they (to put it mildly) did not care to see him address himself to me.

It was not a pleasant position.

Young ladies may be, and are, excused from taking any but a slight part in men's talk, but they are expected to furnish the music, and be able to accompany a song or sing themselves. But in this household there was no instrument, and not one had the slightest knowledge of music. The same with drawing; while as for discussing a novel, oh!—— So much for their practical and solid education.

The result was, that when this young man came to the house on an evening, he, after a few civilities exchanged with the daughters, came through into the warehouse, and had a discussion with my cousin on theology or politics.

Sometimes my cousin was called away for a few minutes, and I did my best to fill his place till he returned. Flattered with the attention which the schoolmaster showed whilst I was speaking, I secretly resolved to bring myself, if possible, up to his level (except in theology, which I considered then, and do yet, as a question on which men might talk for ever without coming to any conclusion).

To put my thoughts into action, with the few pence I possessed I bought a shilling treatise on algebra, and a sixpenny book of lessons in French.

But I had these only a very short time till they disappeared, and could never be found. Feminine influence, I am sure, was at the back of this. No man could be so small. But I never knew who it was, though I have a pretty good guess.

There were some in the household who looked with a jaundiced eye on the growing intimacy between the stranger and myself.

"Listeners never hear any good of themselves," is a very old saying, and, I have no doubt, a pretty true one; but let the reader ask himself how many books he has read where some one or other of the characters did not accidentally overhear something important about himself.

In real life it occurs every day, and most of the divorce cases with which the evening papers are filled hinge upon some words accidentally overheard, or some tell-tale scrap of paper picked up.

Thus it happened that one evening I was working in the warehouse, and I had occasion to go into the kitchen.

For a wonder, at that hour it was without an occupant, and the door into the front-room was open. Having got what I wanted, I was coming out, when I became conscious of two voices in the front-room. One of them—a feminine voice —I recognized directly, and the other was that of the stranger.

The first voice said something about myself (I will only say it was not flattering).

Dead silence ensued.

The very same words were repeated, and with the same result. The stranger was not to be drawn, and the owner of the feminine voice changed the conversation.

I can't say that I was much surprised, but I certainly was pleased with the silence of the stranger.

Whatever was the reason I don't know, but after that time I saw very little of him, and several things, small in themselves, but significant, and all pointing in the same direction, led me to the conclusion that he thought it best to avoid me.

I was now less frequently on the road and more in the warehouse, and yet I could get no time to study.

But the lessons of Benjamin Franklin had taken effect, and I was more than ever determined to keep my own counsel, and stand entirely on my own feet.

Hitherto one of the reasons that had kept me from leaving was the company of the stranger: that was gone. Another reason was the difficulty of finding employment without a character; but I called to mind the masons employed on the extensions of the premises, and my exchange of views with them. They never carried recommendations when seeking employment, and, above all, they worked short hours, and in the open air.

This last circumstance decided my plan of

action. I would go as a builder's labourer; the hours were the same as for the mechanics, and by exercising economy I could live if they could.

About this time the Post-Office Savings Bank was beginning to be known, and I had already placed a few shillings in it. A commercial traveller gave me a five-shilling piece for a Christmas-box, and having scraped a few more shillings together, I had sufficient to pay my train fare to London, and live for one week. If I did not get a job in that week it would be awkward, but I wouldn't think of that.

A few days after the New Year I left, and once more found myself in the great city. I had the address of the people with whom I had stayed for a night or two when I came from Mosston with my Cousin William. This trifling circumstance— what a difference it made in my feelings! So much is said about young people, and the "sharks" that await them on their arrival in London, but here I was, and knew where to go to, and yet be in lodgings. The landlady, a widow, let me have a room to myself (it was right down in the basement) for half a crown a week. Paying a half-crown in advance, I took possession, and felt, for the first time in my life, at home, and yet it was the fact that everyone in the house was a lodger, for the landlady had no family. For the first day or two I wandered about almost without aim; my sensations were so new, and the feeling of absolute freedom—at last—was that delightful, that it entirely took away any feeling of anxiety about work.

But though I lived on bread and coffee, obtained at any of the coffee-houses that were so common, at least in certain parts of London, my few shillings were rapidly melting away. I had seen St. Paul's, Westminster Abbey, London Bridge, and a few other celebrated places, and began to feel anxious about the future. Before describing how I found work, I will just state here a little incident which happened to me, and which has times out of number flashed through my mind (to this day I never think of London but it crops up); and yet it seems so absolutely puerile—at least, the incident itself—that I hesitate to put it down. But I have mentioned it to one or two persons, and they have told me of equally trifling circumstances that occurred to them, and yet left equally as strong an impression on their mind. I was standing looking into a shop window in a poor street, into which I had wandered in the aimless manner of the out-of-work. I have not the slightest idea of what I was looking at, as the shop was of the commonest type of shops to be found in a poor locality. But I became conscious that a woman behind the counter was beckoning me to come in. I felt astonished. What could she want? A host of fancies came into my head. Was she mistaking me for someone else? But she continued to beckon, and I went inside.

I threw a rapid glance round the shop as I

passed through the doorway, but nothing arrested my attention, and I turned to the woman to ask what she wanted. I now got another surprise, for she put an ear-trumpet up to her ear. I think it was the first I had ever seen. I asked her what she wanted, and she said she wanted me to bring up a basket of coals for her from the cellar, that she could not carry them up herself, and that I appeared out of work, and that she would give me fourpence.

Looking round for the entrance to the cellar, she showed me a ring in the floor of the shop. There was no one in the shop but we two, and a crowd of thoughts were in my mind, when, stooping down and lifting up the trap-door, I saw the cellar floor, but no coals. There was a short ladder reaching from the floor of the shop, exactly like what is used on buildings, and called a spar ladder.

Seeing me hesitate, she said, "It's all right." I went down, keeping my eyes open, and saw the basket standing full of coals. Seizing it, I was up the steps in a trice, and closed the trap-door. The woman gave me the fourpence, and I went out of the shop, and passed out of the street. Many a time I wished I had taken the name of the street, but I never found it again.

"Is that all?" I hear the reader say.

Yes, that is all; but why did she give me fourpence for five minutes' work, at the rate of four shillings per hour? And then it seemed such a poor shop; no customer had come out of it while

I was looking in at the window, and no one came in while I was inside, certainly only five minutes. One circumstance dwells on my mind: I am certain that the cellar did not contain one piece of coal, except what was in the basket, and there was plenty of room for that in the shop above. If she had said, "I will give you three-halfpence," I would not have wondered, but fourpence was more than the value of the coals.

At this time the Underground Railway was being pushed on—at least, some part of it—for I rode regularly to work on a part already built. I asked for a job as bricklayer's labourer. A bar was pointed out to me, and I was told the foreman (I remember his name was Gregory) was inside. I went in, and called for a pot of something—most likely stout.

The bar was full: a lot of people who seemed without money were standing back from the counter, and those who had money were talking loudly over their liquor at the counter.

The foreman was among these. I asked him for a labourer's job, and he said I could start next morning. My stout was placed before me; I took one mouthful, but the sharp taste (it was in the pewter) almost took my breath away.

Having got a job, I felt quite satisfied, and, looking round, I noticed a man standing near me with a red nose and a wistful look. I handed him the pot, having only taken one mouthful. He thanked me with an effusion that quite embarrassed me.

My next concern was to buy a shovel, but no

hods were used on this job. Having to be at work next morning by seven o'clock, I hurried back to my lodgings. The landlady thought I was lucky in finding a job so soon, and I slept very little that night for thinking about the morrow.

CHAPTER XI

I START WORK AS A LABOURER TO THE BRICKLAYERS

THIS was in January, 1866. I forget the exact locality of the section on which I was to start, nor can I remember the name of the station where I got out. This, to anybody who knew London, and the system of workmen's tickets which was in vogue at that time, will not be surprising, for the distance made no difference in the price—one shilling per week. I was lodging in the West End, and I think Praed Street was the station where I got in to go to my work. Of course, it was not daylight at seven, but for outdoor brick-work it was made to do.

The first morning I was very hungry by twelve o'clock, for we never stopped for breakfast. When noon came we rushed in all directions to get our dinners; I went to a coffee-shop and got a beef-steak pudding for fourpence. These are called pot-pies in some parts of England. One of my comrades said to me, " Now, young fellow, don't let them see you are from the country, but say, 'Give me a slice of plum.'" This was plum pudding cut into slices about an inch thick—one penny.

My work was wheeling and stacking bricks. The bricklayers appeared to me, at that time, almost as demigods, the way they shouted for mortar or bricks and the difference between their treatment and ours by the boss.

I soon found there were no men on the job, only "blokes." In the morning it was beautiful to see it breaking daylight, and during the day we were enlivened with music from the street organs.

One particular tune at that time, always joined in at the last line by the men, was "Come and have a lark with the jolly butcher-boy."

I soon found there were only three subjects upon which these "blokes" could or would talk: beer, music-halls, and women. They were all jolly fellows, and full of chaff, saying to me, "I suppose you will be writing to your friends in the country to come up." The strangest thing to me at that time was, that they were all, without exception, from the country, and I have found it so all through life.

Let anyone go on to any job to-day in any big provincial town or city, and it will be strange if he can find 5 per cent. of the workmen to belong to a town or city.

All the able-bodied joiners, masons, bricklayers, and labourers are from the country, either English, Irish, or Scotch. If they settle in a town, their sons want to be clerks, cashiers, or something where they will not have to take off their coats.

A delusion.

Hard work strengthens a man, if he is fed, and gets to bed at night in anything like proper time. I never felt better in my life than when working on this job; and let me say that it was no child's-play, wheeling bricks. The men, I could see, rather thought I was too slight in build to manage this, but I had no trouble, not even at the first.

The job was all hoarded in like a great railway yard, and about the only things we could see were the splendidly written public-house signs, over the tops of the hoardings. Whenever we went out of the gates to meals there was a string of lads and men standing. "Have you a farthing?"

At first I wondered, but there was a place close by where splendid soup could be had for a penny, though whether a pint or a quart I forget. Asking one of these fellows what he wanted a farthing for, he showed me a halfpenny in his hand, and said he was trying to make up a penny for soup.

From reasons to follow, I think it must have been about King's Cross where I started to work. When the workmen said Clapham, Islington, Fulham, and so on, I had not the slightest idea of where these places began or ended.

During meal-times it was my practice to look at the posters on the hoardings round the works. I remember well the dramatic scenes from Charles Reade's "Never Too Late to Mend," though whether he dramatized it himself or not I forget now. About as many posters were devoted to the "Master of Ravenswood," an adaptation of the "Bride of Lammermoor," "I bide my time" striking the eye continually.

About the only literary poster that I recall was one representing some entirely unpractical craft with *Argosy* in huge letters, and the accompanying legend, "Freighted with golden grain."

When Saturday came the first time, and I got my wages, though Saturday was a lying-on day (I was paid fivepence an hour), I thought I was in Eldorado. We were paid at midday, and I determined to walk up Oxford Street to Edgware Road in the clear January sunshine, though I had workman's tickets in my pocket. I had some money, and, what was more, had work to go to on Monday, and I thought I deserved a slight treat. I passed a book-shop which had a box on the pavement beside the door, with a lot of unsaleable stuff at a penny or twopence each.

Turning some over, I saw a French book by Lamartine, which had no backs, but was otherwise in good condition. Securing this, the next thing was to get a dictionary. I got a small one, second-hand, for a shilling; how the bookseller must have laughed after I was gone—twopence at the most was its value.

I felt fit up, and the next thing was to try my new tools. By this time I knew where there were coffee-shops, where a working man could sit for a little bit over his refreshments. Entering one of these, and calling for a pot of coffee and something to eat, I seated myself in a corner at a table and commenced to eat.

As soon as I saw that no one was paying any attention to me, I laid my Lamartine on the table and made a start. Plenty of young fellows read "Black Bess, or the Knight of the Road," at meal-times, and no one could tell but what I was doing the same thing, as my copy had no backs.

Emboldened, I kept the small dictionary in my hand, and sought to make out what to me was almost a cryptogram. Alas! after a few words I came to *que*, and that not in a place where the context explained its meaning. I was defeated, and gave up the French, never taking it up again for about ten or twelve years.

I passed out again into the bright sunshine, and reached Edgware Road about three o'clock. A bootblack hailed me at the corner, and I got my shoes blacked. Whilst standing with my foot on the block, a young fellow came past and said cheerily, "Now, Bricky, getting a shine, eh?" What! I, the sport of fate, in London only a fort-night, and standing in the glorious sunshine with my wages in my pocket, and taken for a brick-layer? What was Lamartine? what was any-thing? I was free; I was independent. I had not then heard the phrase, "You're away with it now," or I would have said so to myself.

It was only after I had entered into my lodgings that a slight reaction after this excitement began to manifest itself. After paying my landlady, the little room seemed dull and prison-like by daylight; this was Saturday, and about half-past three o'clock in the afternoon. Washing myself and putting on the few clothes I had for change, I went out and spent the whole evening to a late hour walking about Edgware Road, which at that time was like a fair on Saturday nights. The Saturday previous I had not yet obtained work, and therefore was keeping quiet in the lodgings; but now I enjoyed to the full this gigantic shifting kaleidoscope of humanity.

I recall one young man who stood in the gutter and played a concertina; a little girl was with him. Both seemed to shrink from asking for money, merely taking what (it was not much) was given them. I thought to myself, " Well, your position is certainly worse than mine." I bought some little things of some of the numerous vendors of toys and penny articles, and finally went home to bed.

The next day, Sunday, was an awful dull day for me; bars were not to be thought of. I put a lot of time in walking about Hyde Park, but, do what I would, Sundays were always miserable during my stay in London. I tried the church, only to be told twice that I must come out of the pew I had entered. Like the majority of working men, I have always considered that Radicalism, or at least Liberalism, was the only policy for such as I; but I shall ever be grateful to the Conservatives for allowing the British Museum to be opened on Sundays. I say " allowing," for Balfour, I am certain, could have prevented it, but he chose to let it be taken as a non-party question.

Had it only been open when I was there, how gladly the boon would have been enjoyed! But a sudden and almost startling change was impending, though I knew it not—a change that permitted me to see the Museum and the National Picture Gallery during the day at my leisure, and yet not lose my employment.

The change came about in this manner: After I had been working a fortnight from seven in the morning till five in the evening, a squad was picked out to build a part of the tunnel in lengths. A tunnel, be it understood, is not necessarily a hole bored through a solid, like the latest London tubes. I speak of '66 and the old underground. If two parallel brick walls are put up for, say, thirty feet, or any amount of feet, in an open field, and the space between these walls arched over, and then the whole lot covered over with soil; if, I say, a road passes through, or a footpath even, the place would be spoken of as a tunnel, and anyone would say, "I went by way of the tunnel" or "through the tunnel," and speak as correctly as if he had gone through a hole bored or drilled out.

Why I have said all this is because I have almost exactly described the work that this squad was going to do. The only difference is that no ordinary road was going through, but a railroad; and therefore, instead of the two parallel brick walls being started on ordinary foundations, an inverted arch consisting of several rings of brickwork was first put in, and the side walls carried up in continuation to the requisite height. Then there was an interval whilst the carpenters came and put in the centring, and finally the squad of bricklayers came back and arched over the length in question.

As I was only a labourer, I can't say what was the length of tunnel put in at a time, but of course, to suit the battens, they would be all alike; but I well remember the startling (to me) change in the hours.

I don't know whether the bricklayers were on piece or not. I asked no questions, but I know my time went on by the hour, with nothing extra for overtime. If the bricklayers were paid over-time, as they often are, first time and a quarter, then time and a half, and sometimes double time, then they must have drawn enormous sums, for, speaking from memory, I am within the mark when I say that two days and a half without stopping was thought nothing.

All through the nights we worked with naphtha lamps, and we stopped every five hours for one hour. If anyone wanted money he could get "sub."

What a boon the London coffee-houses were! I had nothing to carry; just went into them every five hours, and had something to eat. We were like a squad of men making bricks: each man had his post.

Many times I wondered why I was picked out, but perhaps sobriety had something to do with it. Now I come to how I could see the Museum and the other sights through the day at my leisure.

It was while the carpenters were putting in the centring. The whole thing worked out like this: A huge ditch or cutting was to be seen with a network of shoring to keep the sides from falling in.

We went in; the bricklayers put in the inverted arch at the bottom of the cutting, and carried up the side walls to the proper height.

This was a long shift, and varied tremendously in the time taken, according to the nature of the ground forming the sides of the cutting; if it was treacherous, then there was a lot more shoring to remove as we gradually built up. Still, we never stopped except for one hour every five till this was done.

If the Employers' Liability Act had been in operation, then we would not have been allowed to work as long. Many a time I was so sleepy I could scarcely put a bite into my mouth. The carpenters used to be long enough at their part of the work to give us time to go home and sleep, and then take a day.

Though the work was heavy, I enjoyed it, and employed the off-days to go and see the sights, as I have said. I made good use of my time, and put all the money in the Post-Office Savings Bank that was left after paying for everything.

The air was always very chilly when the day broke, and we gladly extinguished the naphtha lamps. Our second shift after the centring was placed was much shorter.

After a few lengths had been put in like this we gained upon the excavators, and were put on at regular time—namely, seven till five—at another part of the work. I was hardening every day, and getting thoroughly into condition, when suddenly I was paid off, through no fault of mine.

It came about thus : In the building trades there are set times for changing the hours; but they are not always the same, and sometimes even old hands will ask, What date does the full time start ? or, *vice versâ*, What date does the short time commence ?

The dates are often printed on the union cards, but not always; and bricklayers, joiners, and masons often vary in the winter on the same job.

To-day, while I write, in this district the bricklayers take only half an hour for dinner during the winter, whilst the masons take an hour. Now, as I was new to this system, I did not know when the full time commenced, and coming to work as usual at seven o'clock, I found the men working and another man in my place. This, I think, was rather sharp practice. However, I simply said that if I had known I would have been on the job prompt.

I got a line from the foreman, and went and got my wages. I now resolved to leave London. I had saved a little money, and was accustomed to the work. I had some letters from the North to the effect that the building trade was brisk. Very little time was needed to pack up my few clothes, and I got a job the day after leaving London.

Whether it was mostly due to the influence of the Limited Liability Act, as I think it was, or not, the fact is the huge manufacturing towns in the North were very busy. I had worked a few months in the North as a labourer when I was thrown into contact with a mason whom I had known as a boy at Mosston.

He suggested that I might try my hand at knocking up blockers, as there was a demand for these, and they did not require much skill. I hesitated at first, but he said he would help me all he could, and even speak to his employer on my behalf.

As he was a great favourite with his employer, my application for a trial was granted. My employer lent me some tools, not many being required, as blockers are mostly done with the hammer, though some have the margins dressed with the mallet and chisel.

This was the method in my case, and in a short time I acquired a tolerable proficiency in the use of the tools.

I now found the benefit of my previous economy, as my wage at this work for a few months was just sufficient to exist on, but left no margin for clothes or tools.

But I was lodging with a widow, who knew what struggling with poverty was, and who laid out my money to the very best advantage.

She told me what I have often heard from

others since—namely, that the lodgers who had the smallest wage, as a rule, were the most regular payers.

Thus the autumn and winter passed without my being obliged to draw all my little capital. The winter was pretty open, and I looked forward to the spring and a rise of wages. Being laid off during a sharp frost, I was sitting in the lodgings one afternoon when my employer rapped at the door. On going to the door he told me that if I liked I could come next morning to a small quarry that he rented, and he and I could work at baring the quarry while the frost lasted.

Baring is taking the soil off the top of the stone, and in the small country quarries is generally done in the winter-time, though in the neighbourhood of large towns, and where there is a big demand, it goes on all the year round.

I went in the morning, and my employer was there, but no one else, those who worked there regularly having gone home till the frost ceased.

Perhaps the average reader will pardon me for telling him that stone, if it is green—that is, fresh from its natural bed—or if it is moist, becomes practically unworkable with frost, though very dry old stone may be worked.

Well, when I recall the means and appliances that I found in that quarry and compare them with those of to-day (with the Employers' Liability Act in operation), I don't wonder that some men say that the result of a lot of recent legislation will be that the average workman will become more helpless every year.

I was just watching some men baring in a quarry to-day. They had a gangway at the least four feet broad to wheel their barrows upon, and only one barrow at a time was on the gangway. This means a broad footpath for the man wheeling.

I found in my case one plank not more than six inches broad, and this one plank was cut and grooved with the wear of the old-fashioned narrow wheel of the barrow. The height of the plank would be about twenty feet from the ground, and the barrow had to be tipped on this plank—that is, it was not a question of wheeling over a cutting and then tipping on a broad landing-space.

Certainly the span was not great—about eighteen feet at the most. Well, after the barrow was filled, my employer looked at me as much as to say, " You wheel," and I did.

I was strong enough and active, and managed for about an hour not so badly; but the soil was freezing on the plank, making its surface still more bumpy. The perspiration stood like peas on my forehead in spite of the frost.

My employer, an oldish man, but very strong, said to me : " Why, you're sweating !"

I said : " It'll make anybody sweat keeping that barrow on the plank in the state it's in."

" Let me have a go at it." The barrow was filled, and spitting on his hands, he grasped the handles and set out. He reached the place where he had to tip safely, but, when he tipped the barrow, the wheel skidded, and down he went to the bottom. But one of the legs of the barrow prevented its falling, though it was hanging in a queer position by one leg. I ran down to the bottom and helped him on to his feet; he was practically no worse, hard as nails. Looking up, he said: "Mind the barrow." I secured it, and we packed up, to my great joy.

Falling in with some of his workmen who were walking about, and telling them the whole occurrence, they roared with laughter, saying it was just like him, and served him right.

CHAPTER XII

THE OLD MAN SHOWS HIS HAND

THE winter passed slowly but surely, and the spring came. I was looking to it with the utmost eagerness. My small capital was severely tried with the broken weather, and although I was making great progress at the trade, it was no use asking for a rise in the winter.

After all, the building trade is a season trade, and many people who have property that really requires alterations or repairs wait till the fine weather comes to get it done. But "while the grass is growing the horse is starving," is an old saying.

Just when I was going to ask my employer for an advance, I was taken aback in this way: There was a small shooting-box on some hills a few miles from where I was working, and my employer was going to carry out some slight alterations at it. He didn't tell me at first that this would involve a long walk night and morning, and that he was taking me because the old hands were rather *too old* to do this without wanting something extra.

He himself was what is called a "waller"—that is,

he did not dress stones, but set them on the walls when dressed, or else built walls of rough, un-hewn stone. He had a foreman, who looked after the men who dressed the stones, called "banker hands," from the bench or banker on which stones are dressed.

This foreman, under whose eye I had hitherto worked, was a quiet man, clever at his work; in fact, it was the old tale—one had the brains, the other the money.

This shooting-box was only two and a half miles from my employer's house in the country, and he told me I could lodge with him for the few weeks the job would last. This was all very good; my lodgings would cost him nothing, and at this job I could do as much as a journeyman.

But I was depending on his foreman's word to get an advance, because he himself would say, " I leave the banker hands to my foreman." I foresaw complications, but said to myself, " It is only for a few weeks, and I will save the lodging money, and when the job is finished the season will be further advanced, and I shall be in a better position to ask for more money."

Telling some of the workmen that I was going to lodge with the " old man," as we called him, they laughed, and looked at each other signifi-cantly.

One who was very friendly with me said : " Your rise is ——d for a bit; mind what you're doing. If you were here you'd be all right, but out there he'll have it all his own way.

"There is a big job going on here, where they are paying two shillings a week more than the wages, and if the old man had asked any of us old hands to go out yonder, and pay lodgings, we would all pick up, and go to this new job. But the old man is getting all you young fellows to go."

I knew that every word of this was true, but I was not independent like this old hand. So we went on the Monday morning following this conversation, the old man, my friend from Mosston, another apprentice, and myself.

I soon found out why all the young hands were picked out. The old man knew a thing or two. The shooting-box was on a hill-side by itself, and, although it was two and a half miles' walk from my employer's house, he called us up every morning himself, so that we had to be on the job at the exact time.

Of course, he could not alter the hours, but one of us had to sharpen the picks and chisels at night, as there was no blacksmith's shop near at hand.

Then it was still very cold in the mornings, and as we had to carry these picks and chisels, as well as our cans full of tea or coffee, we could not get our hands in our pockets, and they used to be numb, with cold steel always in contact with them.

The old man had a small forge, and the Mosston man had to sharpen the picks and chisels. He cursed the job, saying it would be the last time that he would be roped in like this.

My job at night was to blow the bellows, and the other apprentice, who lodged along with the Mosston man, used to laugh at us both.

The old man had heard about my raising a laugh at his wheelbarrow performance, and as I had managed to run the plank for an hour without falling, this apprentice, who was a bit of a wag, christened me " Blondin."

What a true saying it is, " You must live with people to know them." I got to know the old man in a fortnight, with lodging with him, but without that I might have worked years for him and not have known him.

The job was not a big one, some alterations to the stables and outbuildings, and we only used very little new stone in it, as we worked up a lot of the old stone.

I found myself doing most of the labouring work, but there was no help for it, and the waggish apprentice did his share.

I was carrying a biggish stone up the gangway one day, which the Mosston man had worked. There was a good bit of trade in it, as we used to say—that is, it required a skilled hand to work it. Coming up the gangway, the old man said :

" Mind and don't let that stone fall, for if it breaks you can't work another one."

This was the first intimation that he was trying to get straight with me for the wheelbarrow incident. It was a mean remark, for the Mosston man had been as many years at the trade as I had months.

I said nothing, but waited my time, knowing that I was doing very well; in fact, Mosston said I was going to be a regular "H—ll Fire Jack."

At nights I could not find a book in the house to read, but one night the old man was writing a letter, and he said to me, " How do you spell —— ?" and he mentioned a local place-name. I spelt it, and he said, "Right," but didn't try me with another one.

A few days after this I got into a scrape, that sent the wheelbarrow incident entirely into the background.

Every morning I took all our cans into the house to be warmed for breakfast, and brought them out again at eight o'clock. The owner of the place was absent during alterations, and the only people in the house were an old woman and a young servant, who, I believe, was either a daughter or niece of the old woman.

The door by which I had entered had a window on the right, and another on the left. The window on the left was the kitchen window, and the one on the right was that of a room which I had never entered, or, indeed, ever looked into. But in this room a very old man lay dying, though I was not aware of his existence.

Nobody had ever mentioned him, and as he had no disease, but was just dying of old age, and there being no doctor (at least, while I had been there) in attendance, there was none of that anxious going to and fro that denotes illness.

Close to the door, but on the right-hand side, in front of this right-hand window, was a dog-kennel, in which a large Pomeranian dog, belonging to the owners of the lodge, was kept, and chained during the night.

I say "belonging to the owners of the lodge," for, as will be shown, this is important. This dog used to pull at his chain and bark every morning when I took the cans in to be warmed. Still, he did not look a naturally ferocious dog, and after a time or two I did not pay a great deal of attention to him in passing in and out.

But one Monday morning, in taking in the cans, he never showed himself or barked. I noticed this, but as he looked rather lethargic than savage, I thought he had got accustomed to me and looked upon me as one of the household.

(A well-bred dog soon knows a workman.) Going then boldly in, I found the two women standing close to the kitchen table, which was placed with one end close to the door by which I entered, and their skirts prevented me from seeing in below the table.

I was standing, waiting for the young woman to take the cans, when the dog suddenly, without a sound, crept from under the table, and sprang at my throat.

They had chained him to the leg of the table, and luckily I was just an inch too far for him to bite me. There was a commotion, and instead of taking them to task for having their master's dog where he could seize an innocent person unawares, I did a very foolish thing.

I said nothing to the men when I went back, as I knew I should only be laughed at.

But next morning, in going with the cans, I picked up a smooth stone almost as big as a half-brick, and carried it in my right hand.

Out came the dog from his kennel, and received the stone right between the eyes.

Will it be believed? the stone rebounded off his head and went right through the window, smashing a bottle that stood on the window-sill, and sending the fragments over the old man lying in bed.

I slipped into the kitchen, placed the cans down on the table, and out again to my work as quickly as possible.

Very soon out came the old woman, and went straight up to the old man. I was very busy, but saw out of the corner of my eye. They turned round, and the old man called on me to come to them. On my approaching them the old woman started in this manner.

I was a housebreaker.

She'd give me seven years.

Did I know that flinging stones at a watchdog was the same as burglary? What she would do; and then I had very nearly sent the invalid into his grave with fear.

The old man's face was a study whilst the stream of words was flowing. He looked from one to the other, not knowing what line to take, as my labour was valuable to him.

When the old woman slackened up to take breath, I took the chance of speaking. Briefly, what I said was to the effect that I had not the slightest idea that anyone was ill in the house, and that I was very sorry for any disturbance to the invalid. I also was willing to get another pane put in at once at my expense. Then, seeing the old man's face lighten up a bit, I turned to the indignant dame and began:

"You have a lot to say about courts and burglary and watchdogs, but how about yourself? The dog is not yours, and its place is in the kennel, and not chained to the table-leg behind the door to seize any innocent person by the throat on entering.

"When I am brought up for attacking a watchdog, you will have to answer the charge of taking him from his kennel, and putting him behind the door for a trap," etc. etc.

The old man saw his way at once. "Yes, mistress, the lad is right there; the dog should have been in the kennel. I'll see that the glass is put in at once, and I'll tell him to take care in the future."

The old woman went away very quietly. I had a long walk that night to get a pane of glass, which cost me fourpence, and nothing more was said, but from that time the dog never barked when he saw me.

The job did not last much longer; but when I

got back to my old lodgings, I found that two strangers who had come to work (at the job where they were paying two shillings a week more than the wages) had heard the tale, with sundry embellishments, from the waggish apprentice.

I don't know whether the landlady had been speaking to them about me or not, but after a little chaff, about who frightened the old man to death, the conversation turned upon my employer.

It seems he had been going about railing against their boss, who, not content with coming from a distance and taking a big contract, had raised the wages two shillings per week.

The result was my employer's best men had started on the new job, and one offered to get me a start at six shillings a week more than I was earning.

Besides this, the work was of a very much higher class than any ordinary building.

After a look at the new building, I saw that I could manage to dress the ashlar and quoins, and started on the Monday, after giving notice on the Saturday for my back time.

My old employer looked very sour, but said nothing.

I was astonished at this, but, as I said, he knew a thing or two.

After working all the week on the new building, I went for my back time to my old job, which was only two hundred yards distant, when a disagreeable surprise was waiting for me.

7

At that time, although wages were always spoken of as so much per week, all the building trades in this district were paid once a fortnight.

As I had left my old employer on the Saturday before the pay Saturday, I was entitled to a week's wage.

I saw the men looking at one another, and the old man studiously avoiding my eye. Waiting till all the men had been paid, I went into the cabin.

The old man looked at me.

" What do you want ?"

" I want my wages."

" You'll get them when you come back to your work."

" Why didn't you say that when you got my notice last week ?"

" That's my business."

I knew his style by that time, and that words would simply be wasted on him. So, telling him he would hear about it, I came out again. I told the widow, my landlady, that her money would be all right in a few days, and took out a County Court summons for my money.

This was before the Act of 1875.

But the old man was ready for me, and I got a summons for six weeks' lodging money.

As I had no writing to show that he was to pay my lodgings at this outside job, if I had gone to court I would have won, and lost, and the six weeks' lodgings were more than my one week's wage.

The old man and I met before the court day. We agreed to let the thing drop. The law was satisfied, as the two summonses were paid for, and I didn't regret not being presented at court.

I had, however, the satisfaction of six shillings a week advance.

CHAPTER XIII

I BECOME A JOURNEYMAN

I was now fairly launched in the building trade. My new job was a large building, and there was quite a gathering of masons from all parts. Some of them had tramped all over England and the greater part of Scotland.

It was really interesting to hear their experiences, though some of them were about how they had " sloped " their lodgings, and the greater part of them just anecdotes of the various shifts they had been put to on tramp to raise the wind.

Still, they were fine, jolly fellows, and told their tales with effect, and the work went full swing all the time.

During the meal-hours the best fun was to hear the masons telling tales at the expense of the joiners. These in their turn would have a go at the bricklayers or plasterers, whilst all hands relished a poke at the plumbers. The labourers used to have some laughable yarns, where some witty Irish labourer was sure to be the hero. The most telling yarns were the shortest. I will just mention one or two as specimens.

A mason was setting a stone step down in a cellar. He put the level on the step, but as it was rather dark in the cellar, he brought the level up into the street to see it.

Another old mason got a job to lay bricks, but the boss said to him: "This won't do; you're not breaking joint." "I know," he said, "and how the —— can I when the bricks are all one length?"

One joiner served seven years in one yard, and his boss said: "Here, I'll give you a pound if you'll go away and don't tell anyone where you served your time."

"Right."

He went to another town for employment. A builder said to him: "Can you make window-sashes."

"Yes."

"Well, you can start to-morrow."

He started, and worked at a sash till he was sick of it, and covered it up with shavings under the bench. Then he started with number two, which was a little better. The boss looked in.

"What's that you're making?"

"A sash."

"A sash?"

"I've never seen anything like it in my life."

The joiner saw he was done anyhow, so he said: "You needn't take such a tone; I'll bet you had worse than this made in your shop."

"Not a bit of it; my youngest apprentice could make better."

"I'll bet you a pound you have."

"Done."

The joiner planted the pound he had from his late employer. The new boss covered it with another. Then the joiner pulled out sash number one from beneath the bench. Tableau!

I worked about six months on this building, and the time flew fast. Then, thinking I could get more money, I left, and got a job about forty miles from the last one. I stayed with my new employer two years, and at the end of that time got the full wages.

I have said that my first initiation into the craft began by knocking up blockers in the autumn of 1866. I have never kept records of the exact day of any of these events, but have always been content with knowing the month and year.

I remember well my first start for full wages. It was in the late autumn of 1869, so that I had qualified for a journeyman in three years. As at that time we were not paid by the hour, but by the week, my first journeyman's wages were twenty-four shillings per week, as the winter hours had commenced; if it had been summer, they would have been twenty-seven.

A very few words on the technics of the trade, now that my experience is that of a journeyman. The ordinary reader has no idea of the skill required to cut all the common varieties of free-stone quickly and cleanly. It is really a question of maxima and minima. If the workman tries to take too much off at once, he will have his work full of holes and ragged edges. If, to make a clean job, he takes a light hold, he is too slow, and will soon be told so.

Most people speak of stone as hard, but that does not give so much trouble as its brittleness. A glance at any building will soon show this. If there are any particular parts that project, note how the corners are broken off and the edges chipped. When a stone is turned on the banker, old bags have to be put as softening, or all the edges will be snipped. That commonest of all ornament, a chamfer, had its origin from this difficulty. A chamfer substitutes an obtuse angle for a right angle.

When I started on my second job at fourteen shillings a week, I started on ashlar. Ashlar is to a stone wall what a brick is to a brick wall. We say "a brick," but we don't say "an ashlar"; we say "a piece of ashlar." That is because a brick is a standard length, but a piece of ashlar may be one foot long or four feet six inches long, or any length in between.

After three months on this ashlar, I was set to work on stone quoins, which was a step forward, for they have to fit on two different faces.

Next I was set on moulded string course, between the sills. When I left this second job for another forty miles distant, I got the same money, but shorter hours. Instead of working till half-past five at night, I worked till five. As this was a country job, I had more variety of work, from heads and sills to tracery. As this last word is rather a big word in the trade, and is thought, even by journeymen, to be something, I will close my remarks on the art of stone-cutting by saying that by tracery is generally understood the flowing patterns in church and cathedral windows.

A slab of stone the necessary thickness is laid on the banker, and a full-sized pattern in sheet zinc is laid on the stone. One or two men hold the zinc steady, and the workman runs round the pattern with a sharp-pointed tool called a scriber. This scriber ploughs a minute furrow in the stone, and the workman runs along this furrow with a piece of black slate (split very thin). This makes a fine line, and the line, being in this minute furrow, is safe from being rubbed out by the workman's clothes.

By means of centre lines the workman traces the pattern exactly in the proper position on the other side of the slab, and tests this with a steel square. The pattern once properly traced in on both sides of the stone, the main difficulty is overcome, and hence the word "tracery."

After I had been with my new employer a year, he raised my wages to eighteen shillings, and after another year I started as a journeyman at twenty-four shillings, as I have already stated. During these two years I was in pretty easy circumstances, and began to reap the benefit of my efforts. I began the study of music, and took lessons on the violin. My music-master was a painstaking teacher, and he became my friend for life.

These two years flew by on gilded wings,

sometimes working in the country in the summer months, getting the benefit of the fresh air and sunshine. On one of these jobs a rather curious incident occurred, although I daresay I was the only one who ever kept it in my mind, for a certain reason known only to myself.

We were working on a small Catholic chapel, where there was a lot of good work, and this time the architect looked very closely after the masonry.

One day he rode out to the job on a grey pony, or cob, as some would call it. Whilst he was inspecting the work on the scaffold, my employer came to me and said: " You might hold this pony a bit, as all the labourers are engaged."

I went out of the shed in which we were working, and took hold of the bridle, and commenced to walk up and down so that he would not be chilled, as he was rather heated. Meantime my employer was on the scaffold with the architect.

There were three more banker hands working in the shed, who were all too busy to take any notice of anything outside of the shed itself. As there was not much room, bricks and stones and timber being in heaps all over the ground, I stopped at one place, and ceased to walk the pony.

Immediately he wheeled round and set himself in front of me, and looked at me with the most human, and most intelligent human, expression. It was as if he was saying, " I'll look through you."

" Nonsense !" I hear the reader say.

"What bosh! You must have been unstrung."

Well, there was no nonsense; he put his head as close as he could into my face, and looked at me as if he was trying to hypnotize, or, as we said then, mesmerize me.

I really felt queer, but I knew that if I said anything to anyone on the job they would all laugh at me, and I would never hear the last of it. I said to myself that there was nothing strange about his behaviour whilst he was walking about, and resolved to keep him walking, even if it was over bricks, stones, or anything in the way. This I did, and had no further trouble with him.

Well, if the matter had ended here I would never have put it down, but shortly after the architect came again on the same animal. This time he was given in charge of a huge labourer named Barney.

Determined to watch results, I tried to keep Barney in the corner of my eye, but there was someone watching us masons, and the result was that I had to mind my work too closely to keep Barney in view.

On a sudden we heard a shout. Looking up, there was Barney on his back, and his legs in the air. The pony set off at a gallop, the stirrups flapping, all hands running and shouting. The pony was caught and brought back. One of the men said to Barney: "What the h—ll set you to let the pony run away?" Barney said: "He looked at me so."

Of course, we all had to get back at once to our work, and the matter ended there. Many a time since I wished that I had had an explanation with Barney. I have stated all, and exactly all, about this affair, and leave it to the reader's judgment. There are more things in animals' heads than we think.

The woman I lodged with at this time had a little dog that did not seem to know much, but it knew the pay Saturday, and sat near the door waiting for Archie, one of the widow's sons, who came home once a fortnight. If anyone said: "Here's Archie," it made a rush to meet him, but on the other Saturdays he would take no notice, though many a one tried him.

I made a point of lodging always on the outskirts of the towns. By so doing I was saved a lot of walking, and as most of the new jobs were in the suburbs, sometimes for months I would only be fairly in the towns on the Saturday afternoons and evenings.

In the densely populated industrial centres thousands of working men pour into the towns, and spend a lot of money, and go home in high feather, and loaded with purchases. Sometimes the suburban trains were filled with men drunk and fighting, and women screaming, but in general the crowd on a Saturday night was a jolly though noisy one.

I can't help relating a thing that happened to myself and two other young fellows going into town one Saturday afternoon.

Let me first state that invariably if anything occurred out of the usual run, and more than one or two were present, all hands just looked at each other, but never—never, I say—attempted to explain, or even comment on, the event.

I mention this because I have tried to get an opinion from my mates on certain unusual incidents which I knew they had seen from beginning to end, but always in vain. They seemed to me to have a horror of theorizing, or being thought dreamers.

This time there were three of us. My two mates were lively, good-natured fellows from Manchester. We were working three or four miles from a small, but ancient, city, though we always spoke of it as the town. Neither of us belonged to the district, but we knew the locality pretty well, having worked in it for some time.

The city was practically all on one side of a small river, though there was a public-house, and perhaps one or two houses, on the other side. The road by which we came led over a fine old stone bridge into the city, then up a short rise into the market-place.

One or two different routes diverged from this market-place, but one was a continuation of the road by which we came, and the market-place was quite small enough to enable anyone to recognize any familiar figure across its whole breadth.

Without swimming or flying it was impossible to enter the city by the road we came, except the one way over the bridge. The public-house stood on the top of a steep bank, and the road down this bank had high stone walls on each side. As I say, the city was very small, and from the side we came there were practically no foot-passengers except ourselves that afternoon.

It was a fine summer afternoon, and my mates were in the highest spirits. Young, single, and with their wages in their pockets, they had no thought but to enjoy themselves. We walked for about three miles without stopping, and were just approaching the public-house on the top of the bank, when we were joined by a man, apparently a quarryman by his clothes, who we at once put down to be going into the town on the same errand as ourselves.

After a few words about the weather, and so on, we all turned into the pub for a drink. If we had not been so near to the inn, it is probable that my mates, harum-scarum though they were, would have remarked, as soon as myself, certain peculiarities about the stranger, and perhaps not have invited him so readily to have a drink with them.

He was tall, and appeared very tall from his being very thin, though in perfect health. What his coat was like I forget, but he wore a waistcoat and trousers of moleskin, yellow with stone dust, and he appeared to have been working that morning, and have delayed going into the town over some beer, as he was unwashed.

We thought that he lived in the town, as we

could see at a glance that he had never tidied himself after work. He had a short body, and a very small head for his size, and appeared to be about forty. His face was marked with some blue scars, and as he wore neither beard nor moustache, they were very visible. Looking at him I thought of the nursery rhyme :

> " Long legs, crooked thighs,
> Little head, and no eyes."

I didn't like his look, but there was no time for reflection. We all went in and ordered drinks There were only one or two customers in the bar. The weather was warm, and we each drank off one glass of beer and had them filled again. Before we had drank the second the stranger had attracted the attention both of my two mates and the one or two customers already in when we entered.

I can't remember anything that he said, but he seemed to flit—that is the word—about the bar, instead of standing beside his glass. He went first to one end, then to another, then stood in front of the fireplace; and his tall, strange figure, small head, and short body had something positively uncanny about them.

I could see all hands were impressed, but each looked at the other and said nothing.

One thing I recall distinctly : his movements were almost noiseless. It was his short flights (for they were almost like flights, so quiet were they) that disturbed the customers. I could see that, as they stood up to the bar counter, they were uneasy when he passed behind them, and that they watched him out of the corners of their eyes.

I looked at the eldest of my two mates, and said: " I am going into the yard for a minute."

He took the hint, and the three of us went into the back-yard. No sooner were we outside than my mate said : " What do you think of that —— ?"

I said: " Let's give him the slip and talk after."

We rushed down the bank and over the bridge, then walked as fast as we could up the bank on the other side, and through the market-place, following on the same direction, intent solely on putting as much space as possible between us and the stranger. Every now and then I gave a glance behind, but saw no trace of him.

As the direction we were going was taking us uphill, although the gradient was regular and not very steep, we slackened our pace a little to take breath. Two women were immediately in front of us, carrying a large box by the handles, one on each side. They were evidently mother and daughter, and as they were going in the same direction as we were, we did not immediately pass them, for my two mates were amused at their conversation.

The daughter was saying that she was tired, and anyhow they must change hands, as the iron handle of the box was cutting her hand. The mother replied, saying that if they didn't look sharp they would miss the bus that was going to S——, a village a few miles out of the city.

We immediately offered to give them a hand, and two of us grasping the box set off at a good rate, as it just suited the direction we were taking, and was fine fun for the two young fellows. We gathered from the two women that the young one was going out to service, and the mother was seeing her off and helping her with her box.

We soon reached the place where the bus was standing just ready for starting. It was a public-house on the outskirts of the city, and I should say about a mile and a quarter from the one where we had left the stranger, in almost a straight line through the city, which, as I have stated, was a very small one.

The mother thanked us effusively, saying that without our help they would not have been able 'to catch the bus, as they were getting tired. Then suddenly she asked if we would have a glass of beer. We said that it was no trouble, but a pleasure, to help the ladies, and that we would take a glass of beer, but would not think of letting her pay for it, as we were all single young fellows working for good wages.

Accordingly we all went inside. It was rather an old-fashioned public-house, with low ceilings and stone-flagged floor. As we entered there was the usual public-house roar, for by this time it was late in the Saturday afternoon. It was rather dark in the room, owing to the low windows and the tobacco-smoke; but it was not that dark but that we saw something that startled us, and as for myself, I was never so taken aback in my life.

Seated on a chair by a three-legged table, with his beer before him, was the stranger that we had been doing our best to slip. The three of us stopped short and stared at him.

He rose and came towards us without speaking. I don't know what I should have done or said, but the eldest one of my two mates said to him: "You're a nice —— to give us the slip like that; here we've followed you all over the town; you can go and drink by yourself now." And he turned on his heel and went out again, followed by myself and the other young fellow.

I think I hear the reader: "What did the stranger say to that?" Well, he simply said nothing

When we were outside I began to ask my mates what they thought of the affair; but after a few vague remarks, such as "Well, that beats all!" they relapsed into silence and never again referred to the matter.

Now, it was certainly possible for the stranger to have followed us all the way, and to have slipped into the pub while we were putting the box into the cart; but practically it was impossible.

There was only the one road, and I had kept looking round. Then it was broad daylight, and the cart was standing before the door of the pub, and even if it had been that the man could have followed us unseen, he did not know that we were

going inside (we had passed all the other pubs);
and, finally, we were all active young fellows and
yet we were blown with our exertions, whilst he,
a man of forty, was sitting perfectly calm and
cool. I give it up as an enigma, and leave it to
the reader to unravel if he can.

CHAPTER XIV

I GO TO CANADA

"Every dog has his day" is an old saying, and it is one that is generally accepted. For some time I enjoyed the ease and freedom of a single young fellow. I never made one systematic effort to improve my mind. I did not altogether waste my wages—indeed, there were a few pounds standing to my credit in the Post-Office Savings Bank—but except when I practised music, my leisure hours were spent in frivolous amusement. But in the spring of 1872 I determined to go to America.

The idea had often occurred to me, but a variety of little circumstances had prevented me from going. As usual, my mind was made up on a sudden. I paid two pounds down at an emigration agent's office, drew out my money from the Post-Office, and went to Liverpool.

I said "spring," but it was only about the 1st of February. I found a lot of all sorts at Liverpool, bound for Canada and the States. Quickly chumming in with one or two, we went round the streets that evening and bought our kit. This cost us ten shillings each, and consisted of a straw mattress, a tin plate and pot, and a knife and fork, which seemed also of tin.

The next morning after breakfast we went down to the landing-stage. We had to wait a considerable time, during which we were quite worried with the importunities of a crowd of vendors of shoelaces and all sorts of little articles.

At last a small tender took us out to the liner that was out in the river. It was the *Prussian* of the Allan line, a stout, seaworthy craft, but not to be compared with the giants of to-day. We chose our bunks, and deposited our kits in them, and then looked all round and satisfied our curiosity.

When meal-times came, we were all anxious to see what the food was like. The printed instructions given us laid a great stress on the potatoes, but they didn't say that the potatoes would not be peeled. This little fact was important, for if they had been peeled, the mud would most likely have been taken away with the peeling. As it was, I was disgusted with them, and although there was plenty of food, yet the way it was served took away my appetite. The only thing I relished was the plumduff on Sundays.

I pass over the voyage briefly. We had a rough passage—sixteen days—but landed safely at Portland in the State of Maine. The last night on board none of us turned in, but sang songs and told jokes, and speculated on what the land would be like when it was daylight. At last we were allowed to land, and we rushed about like a lot of schoolboys.

The first American thing I noticed was the cloth-topped shoes of a couple of men who were standing on the quay. As I was ravenously hungry, we went into a saloon of some description, and we had some cold apple-tart and ale. I always understood that, owing to what was known as the Maine Liquor Law, no beer was to be had, but we got some without any trouble or concealment.

After looking about the place, we inquired when the train went for Toronto, to which place I had booked. It was about two o'clock in the afternoon when we set off. Portland was then the seaboard terminus of the Grand Trunk Line.

It was only a single track, and we were, I think, from the Friday afternoon till six on the Sunday evening doing the distance. Sometimes we were shunted on to a siding, and left there for hours; then we would clatter along at a good rate for a bit, only to slacken up again and make another halt. But we were only emigrants, and I expect were in a special train for such.

Anyhow, the seats were just bare boards, and the whole look of the carriages was of the plainest and poorest description. At first, I was interested in watching the New World from the windows. It looked like a fairy scene. No black smoky factories or towns, just a succession of houses, all of the same pattern, built of cream-coloured clapboard, with green window-shutters.

This and the unending snow surface, broken only by the dark green of the pine-trees, was lit up with a bright but frosty sun in a sky of blue without a cloud. But before I reached Toronto I was heartily tired of the same bright sun and the same cloudless blue sky.

Certainly, when we went through part of the White Mountains we saw some clouds hanging to their sides, but as soon as we had left their vicinity it was the same blue sky.

I was particularly struck with the smart figures of the brakesmen, running along the tops of the railway waggons and setting the brakes. Nothing of interest occurred till we arrived at Montreal, where we had dinner, and had time for a bit of a look round.

It struck me as being a well-built, compact city, and the number of signs with French names showed that we were now in French Canada. We got into the train and crossed the long railway bridge over the St. Lawrence, and then, passing by the north side of Lake Ontario, we reached Toronto at six on Sunday evening.

The place was very quiet, as no liquor was for sale, till a certain hour (eight, I believe) on Monday morning. At last, after having had breakfast on Monday, I turned out to have a look at what was then, and is yet, the great centre for Canadian emigration. I thought the place very quiet and dull. There were horse-cars on one or two of the streets, but there seemed no sign of any rush or vitality.

The whole city was like a small village, compared to some of the manufacturing towns in the North of England, and when I met with any of my fellow-passengers, and compared notes with them, they all seemed downcast and disappointed.

Disappointed I was, certainly, but not downcast, for I was young, single, in excellent health, and with a few pounds in my pocket, and what was more, was determined to take the first job that turned up, no matter what was the nature of the work.

"What everybody says must be true" is an old saying, and everybody said that to succeed in Canada one must refuse no labour if it were only honest. I saw no sign of any stonework—indeed, the season was far too early, and besides, there was very little of it used; all the houses in course of erection were being built of wood.

First of all I procured lodgings with an English family at the west end of King Street. The father of the family had come from London the year before, and had met the same fate that, I am sorry to say, meets a lot to-day. He had come out in the spring, and had obtained work through the summer.

But when the winter fairly set in he was thrown out of work, and only by the strenuous exertions of his wife were the family kept from starvation. When the spring set in, and he tried for his old employment, there were a lot of new emigrants eager for work, and he was crowded out, to die broken-hearted about three months after I landed.

I passed my time for a few days walking about Toronto, looking at everything that struck me as being different from the Old Country, for that I found was the term always used in speaking of England, Ireland, or Scotland. I saw very few things that I thought strange or worthy of note. The wooden side-walks, the flash barbers' shops, and the number of coloured men walking about the streets were rather new to me, and once or twice I saw a real Indian with his snow-shoes under his arm, for they were of no use in the city.

These, I believe, were country postmen. After a few days it began to show signs of returning spring: the sun had a good deal of power in the middle of the day, although we had always a hard frost at night.

In company with one or two other men, Old Country men, like myself, and, like myself, out of work, I was walking along King Street one afternoon, when a man stopped us, and asked if we were looking for work. We all gave the same answer, of course, and then the stranger told us his name, and said he had a quarry at George-town, about thirty miles west of Toronto. The stone was limestone, and he had limekilns there, producing lime, which he sold off the trucks on the railway immediately in front of St. Lawrence Hall. He sold also stone for building purposes, and had his residence in Toronto, and an office on the side of the railway.

He was going out to Georgetown on Monday morning, and, as the season was approaching, was looking for some extra help.

All this was definite and straightforward, but as I was the only one in the group who was single, none of the others could avail themselves of his offer, as the wage would not keep their households in Toronto and pay their board as well in Georgetown.

Accordingly I agreed to meet him at the depot (mustn't say " station " in America) on Monday morning, and go out with him to Georgetown. I was elated, I had got work, and would see a bit of real Canada, not the city, which is the same as here.

We went out to Georgetown on the Monday morning, and I started work at once. The place must have been a very small one, as I only remember one or two houses. My work was filling the limekilns with the raw stone, and filling railway waggons with the lime. It was labouring pure and simple, but I enjoyed the fresh air and the wholesome, plenteous food of Canada.

I lodged with one of the workmen, paying three dollars a week for my board, and soon had saved more than I had spent walking about in Canada looking for work.

The only drawback was the want of a fixed hour for leaving work in the evening. But after I had been there about a month, I think it was, an opening occurred that seemed to offer a more agreeable prospect, and I availed myself of it.

I have said that my new employer sold the lime from the railway in Toronto, but as I had come out so early, the building season had not set in.

But after the season opened there was someone wanted to aid the man in charge on the wharf. The railway ran then on the open road or wharf along the bay, and the waggons stood right in front of St. Lawrence Hall, the public clock in which was our guide.

The man in charge was a well-known and highly respected Englishman, who had been a long time in the service of the firm. He was kept on all the year round, but each spring he had to engage another, to help him through the summer and autumn, till the building season closed.

As he was the trusted employé, he was allowed to pick out a man to suit himself, and his choice fell upon me. He had only one arm, his left having been amputated, but he had a hook fastened in a wooden arm or stump, and if busy he could shovel the lime as well almost as anybody else.

The lime stood in trucks with sloping roofs, that we could open and fold back on themselves. The builders all had accounts with the firm, and just sent their carts to be filled, and Mr. Weaver, the man in charge, wrote out tickets in a little wooden cabin or office.

But we also did a considerable trade with the farmers, and they all paid cash, and I had to keep a sharp look-out for them. If I saw a farmer's waggon coming, I jumped down immediately, and ran to secure him if possible, as there was a rival firm also on the wharf. There were a lot of small customers, who would get a bushel or so for whitewashing and other purposes, and they paid cash.

Mr. Weaver had the power to give me a trifle extra out of this ready cash if I had been fortunate with the farmers, and he carried out this part of the programme punctually, and strictly according to success.

There was a small public-house, or saloon, as they were called, on the left-hand side going up towards Young Street, and in the summer, when we had been well dusted with the lime, he used to take me in and stand one glass of beer, never any more than one a day. Sometimes there would be a slight lull in business, and again sometimes we had to stand till the waggons were shunted.

Standing in the waggons we had a good view over the bay, and as it very seldom rained, the sun shone bright on the wooden side-walks, and sometimes was so hot that a lot of men carried umbrellas to keep its rays from troubling them, though I never felt it burdensome.

CHAPTER XV

I CROSS INTO THE STATES

THE evenings seemed rather dull, as I knew of no library where I could procure books, though I managed to borrow one or two privately. There was not a great deal to be seen walking about, but I sometimes dropped into a saloon which, I think, formed the first story of an hotel in what was then the Rossin Block in King Street.

There was generally a good violinist and pianist at night, who played high-class music.

One evening I was strolling about in that neighbourhood, when I heard the sounds of a fife-and-drum band practising. I forget exactly the locality, but it was not far from what I always looked upon as the centre of the city—namely, the corner of Young and King Streets.

Going inside, there were some young fellows practising, but no regular teacher. Having done a little on the flute and piccolo myself, I asked to have a try, and a fife being handed to me, I played the " Love-knot Quickstep "—at least, that was the name by which it was known to me.

I was asked to join them, as they were practising for a procession on the 12th of July. I was

I CROSS INTO THE STATES

given a copy of the tunes they were getting up, and, as I have said, there being no regular instructor, I promised to give them a careful study at home, ready for the occasion.

They took my address, and the next evening my landlady said that someone had left a large parcel for me.

I was curious to know what it was, and cut the string at once, and behold! a suit of uniform for me to wear at parades and marches.

Amidst loud laughter from the other boarders, I at once started to try them on, but got no farther than the trousers. Like thoughtless young fellows, they had just sent the first suit that came to hand, or perhaps they were all one size.

Anyhow, after getting inside the trousers, I found on drawing them up that I could have buttoned them round my neck.

" Handy for keeping the dust out of your eyes," said one boarder.

" Make a good sleeping-bag in camp," said another.

" You can pawn the rest and still go on parade," said a third. The landlady and the servant roared with laughter at the figure I cut, and suggested that perhaps they had promoted me to drum-major.

This little incident served for amusement for a few days; but before the 12th of July came I was many miles from Toronto, and the Englishmen who boarded with me were scattered in different directions.

I went one Sunday morning with the landlady to hear the Rev. Morley Punshon, a great light among the Methodists, and, I believe, a former President of the Wesleyan Conference in England.

The building in which he preached was dignified with the name of Metropolitan, but neither the building nor the preacher impressed me much. Having said so, the landlady asked me : Was I aware that that was the great Morley Punshon ? in a tone that implied, " You must be an ignoramus."

Inwardly smiling at her faith in the great man, I changed the subject, and asked her how she liked Canada. She said that she preferred England, of course, but that her husband, a bricklayer, had done very well there, and that she was very well satisfied.

They worked harder than in England, but they handled more money, and that sweetened everything

Shortly after this, though I cannot fix the date any nearer than it was June, came the event that was to separate us all for a bit. It was in 1872, and the summer after the great Chicago fire.

A lot of bricklayers were leaving Toronto for Chicago, from whence came tales of fabulous money being earned by bricklayers and labourers. This affected the building trade in Toronto to such an extent that the trade thought it was a favourable chance to go on strike for a nine hours' day.

They worked ten hours in Toronto at that time.

As this was refused by the employers, a strike resulted, and affected the demand for lime to such an extent that Mr. Weaver informed me that circumstances compelled him to discharge me, but that when things were settled I could start again.

I had done so well with this man that had it been in England I would have waited for a settlement before leaving a job where everything had gone so smoothly; but this was Canada, and there no time must be lost in the summer. It is a case of the winter cometh, when no man can work.

Therefore I bade good-bye to my friends in Toronto, not forgetting the drum-and-fife band, and determined to cross the lake to Buffalo, in the New York State. It was the height of summer, and in those days a wooden steamer went twice a day, morning and afternoon, between Toronto and Buffalo.

I got my wages at night, made my arrangements and visited my friends in the next forenoon, and after dinner went down to the wharf and took ticket for Buffalo. I found it rather cool on the lake, and a slight mist prevented me from seeing much, till we entered into the mouth of the Niagara River, which flows into the west end of the lake. I was now approaching the most majestic spectacle perhaps that North America can boast, but I didn't think then that I was going to see a sight that, to me at least, was far more beautiful than the falls themselves—a sight, indeed, that to this day I am astonished never to see described in print amongst the floods of literature about Niagara.

Perhaps Time, which brings so many changes, has done away with the route I followed, or perhaps those who rave about Niagara in print have never gone by boat (always cheaper than train) from Lake Ontario; but whatever is the reason for their silence, I can assure the reader that if ever he has the chance to follow the route I took he will thank me for having pointed out this omission.

The water of the Niagara River where it enters Lake Ontario is pretty smooth, and only the narrowness of the river shows that it is part of the gorge that has been cut by the mighty stream; but only about seven miles from the mouth we had to stop at a little place called Lewiston, on the right bank of the river.

On getting out we had to go up steps to the top of the bank, where there was a small, narrow-gauge railway that ran along the banks, forming the gorge for about fifteen miles, I think, till it joined the ordinary railway; that coming round the lake from Toronto crosses the river by a suspension bridge within sight of the falls.

It was the view down into this gorge from this little railway that ran along the top that took my fancy the most.

The falls themselves are shrouded in mist, and surrounded by all sorts of everyday sights that mar the effect, and then the eye has to turn from the American to the Canadian, or Horse-Shoe Fall, which is the most obscured by mist.

But the gorge below the suspension bridge to Lewiston is clear of mist, and the whole volume of water is pent up in a narrow channel, and tumbles in all directions as it is beaten back by the banks, thus giving the effect of a stormy sea; and the banks, wooded from the bottom to the top, form a green frame to the many-hued waters, except where Queenstown Heights, with Brock's monument on the top, show the naked rock.

All this is seen, moving like a panorama, as the train runs at a moderate pace along this little railway.

I sat entranced, gazing into the gulf, filled with joy at having the privilege of seeing this magnificent spectacle, and to this day I can say I have lived.

On joining the main line, we had to get our baggage examined by customs officers, for we were now crossing into the United States, and then we ran into Buffalo.

I went straight to the house of a bricklayer, who had left Toronto on the first mutterings of a strike, and after some tea and a wash, turned out to look at Buffalo.

The principal thing which struck me at first was the huge Liberty pole at the foot of Niagara Street.

I had not a great deal of time to see the city that night, though the little I saw convinced me that it was a regular go-ahead Yankee place.

There was a splendid free library there known as the Grosvenor, though I did not get to know of it till some time afterwards, but I cannot refrain from mentioning it here.

There was no form to fill; anyone could go in between the bookcases and pick out the books he wanted. The most costly books published in England were to be found there, and the officials were courtesy itself.

The next day I heard that a man was engaging banker hands (known in the States as stone-cutters) for the Lake Shore and Michigan Southern Railway, commonly spoken of as the Lake Shore, which runs from Buffalo round the southern shore of Lake Erie.

The section of the line on which they were wanted was in the neighbourhood of Cleveland, and the headquarters of the gang was Painesville, about twenty-seven miles from Cleveland. I engaged myself to go, and we went that night by train from Buffalo.

We landed at Painesville some time in the morning, and after engaging lodgings (our board was guaranteed by the company) we started work at dinner-time, one o'clock.

Painesville, Ohio, was a beautiful little town; the cream-coloured, clap-board houses on the outskirts of the town were like pictures.

I was now fairly launched among the Yankees (though in Ohio they gave the name of Yankees only to the down-easters), and as it was midsummer the country was in its full pride of leafy growth.

At first I could hardly sleep for the noise of the katydids, which I can compare to nothing but a policeman's whistle run by steam; and as soon as it was daylight the flies prevented further sleep.

I got up early one morning and took a walk round the garden. I thought I would have a look at the tomatoes, which grew to perfection in the neighbourhood. Looking closely at the plants, I saw the most hideous-looking things, like caterpillars, as big as a man's finger, lying on the leaves.

The meals were just like three good English dinners per day, and at the real dinner (especially a little farther on in the season) the choice of vegetables was absolutely bewildering—quinces, stewed plums, cabbage and potatoes, green peas, green corn, and tomatoes all on the table together.

I found the people most favourably disposed towards the English, and the nature of our work on the railway brought us into contact with the farmers, always a picturesque class.

They would come with peaches and water-melons. The peaches grew to an enormous size, and were very cheap, but I used to say you could never get one fully ripe; there was always a hard, unripe part next the branch.

I said to a German farmer (but they were all called Dutch): "How do you know when these water-melons are ripe, as the ones you call ripe are as green on the outside (at least to my eyes) as grass?"

"Oh," he said, "you can tell by the sound, when they are lying on the ground, if you give them a kick with your boot."

It was hot and no mistake. The 4th of July, the great day in the States, came when we had been only a few days in Painesville.

Of course nobody worked, and I took a good look round. The natives struck me as being very tall on the average, but not very stout.

The German element was decidedly more corpulent, and their temper more easy-going— perhaps cause and effect. We had two lads on the job carrying water with oatmeal in it, each getting four shillings (a dollar) a day.

The squad all wore great soft hats, turned down at the brim, or else huge straw hats that we called ten-centers. They also sported white handkerchiefs round their necks, tied so that a point went down at the back, and protected the spine where it was not covered by the shirt.

When we went to dinner we used all to put our hands in our breeches pockets, hot as it was. That was because at each step that we made on the grass a cloud of grasshoppers would rise and fly, perhaps, against the hand—perfectly harmless, but not pleasant.

CHAPTER XVI

LIFE IN THE STATES

THE nature of the work was putting in stone cattle-guards and culverts at various points on the line. The stone was a beautiful freestone from Berea. As the line at that time was only a single track, we had to put down the work so that if the line was widened, which was in contemplation, the culverts, etc., would suit it.

When a stone train came laden with stone in big blocks, then was the time for a real Yankee rush. "All aboard," the foreman would shout, and we rushed on to the flat stone trucks, each man with a steel pinchbar in his hand. Then we levered the blocks forward to the edge of the truck, finally giving them a good shove, so that they would fall far enough forward to leave the line clear.

The boss stood with his watch in his hand, so as to know when to run for a siding and let a train pass. Keeping one eye on the watch and the other on us, he kept shouting : " Lively, boys —hurry up—let her rip." Then his whistle blew, and we all stood braced for the jerk, as the driver started the train for another job farther along the line.

Putting on all he could, the great red-hot wood sparks flew from the funnel, and burnt our arms, as our sleeves were tucked up as far as possible. Anyone who got burnt was laughed at, to take it off his mind. Some good swearing was done, but there was more laughter.

Sometimes we would be three miles on the stone train, from where our jackets, vests, etc., were lying on the grass ; then the chaff started.

" Sandy, somebody will steal your bank-book."

" Brown, that girl's photo 'll be gone when we get back."

" Let it go : it can't be further gone than Brown."

And so on. The Yankees, especially if there was a Dutchman (as they called all the foreigners) in the squad, were full of chaff. A favourite trick of theirs was, after chaffing him to their hearts' content, to say : " Never mind, a Dutchman's as good as a white man, if he keeps himself square, isn't he ?" When the victim said innocently : " Isn't a Dutchman a white man ?" then there was a chorus of : " Oh no, we can't have that."

Leaving chaff out of the question, the broken English of some of the foreigners was really laughable. But in the evenings, when the day's work was over, the foreigners were decidedly more sober than either English, Irish, or Scotch.

I was in a saloon one night in Painesville, and on being asked what I would have, I said : " A glass of port." I noticed the bar-tender looking at me, and a native said: "If you want port you must say 'medicine.'" I said "medicine," and got port.

Curiosity led me to a place of worship one Sunday in Painesville.

I haven't the slightest idea what denomination it was, but most of the audience were fanning themselves with five-cent fans. The organist played "Home, Sweet Home," as an air for one of the hymns, and each time a verse was finished, indulged in a run on the chromatic scale for two octaves.

After working some weeks in the neighbourhood of Painesville, we shifted our quarters farther along the line, and then again to another place whose name I am not quite sure of, but I think either Madison or Willoughby, and I think on the Ashtabula and Youngstown Railway.

By this time autumn was approaching. I was boarding with a farmer who had a small cider-mill, and after I had been there some weeks, he used to send a big stone jar with the waggon which brought our dinner. This jar, filled with sweet cider, made me a great personage in our squad, even the foreman finding an excuse to come where I was working pretty often.

When the autumn began to break up, we had several wet days, and I had used up all the literature I could find in the house. One day the landlady said to me: "You seem a great man for books. Here is one. Can you make anything of it? None of us know anything about it."

It was Bowditch's "Navigation." Bowditch was a Yankee celebrity in his day, and I have no doubt but that the book was an excellent treatise, both theoretical and practical. But the trigonometry and algebra was a sealed book to me then, to say nothing of the knowledge of Euclid implied. My curiosity was excited by a brief description of logarithms in this book, together with the requisite tables. After reading the description, I thought I would try and extract the square root of 4,840 by them. I chose this number as it represented the number of square yards in an acre, and if I found the square root, I, of course, had the length of the side of an acre. But I had not grasped the rule for finding the indices by the numbers and *vice versâ*, and the result was a dead failure.

In a short time the outdoor stone-cutting closed for the season. I had been very much at home with the different people in the States with whom I boarded. I found them most obliging, and always ready to listen to anything about the Old Country.

But sundry business transactions determined me to spend the winter in Toronto, and I knew so many of the English emigrants with whom I had kept up a correspondence. These things, and the fact that I had some money in the Post-Office Savings Bank, settled the matter. I took train to Cleveland, then to Buffalo.

At Buffalo I made a halt, and crossed the Niagara by the steamboat ferry to Fort Erie on the Canadian side. The river here is about two miles wide, and with a current of about seventeen miles per hour. When we cast loose, the steamboat drifted rapidly down-stream, the helmsman steering so as to cross at a very acute angle; then we beat slowly up to Fort Erie on the comparatively calm water close to the shore.

I changed my United States money into Canadian, and came back again to Buffalo, after having deposited the most of my wages in the Post-Office.

After a day or two spent in Buffalo, I took the train to Toronto instead of the boat, which, I believe, had ceased running for the season. Shortly after I arrived I had a pleasant surprise.

The Canadian Government was paying a bonus of five dollars to every individual who had come out that year and had been three months in the country. I had no difficulty in making out my credentials, and walked to the Government House, a big brick building at the west end of Toronto, and was paid in silver five-cent pieces, the official apologizing for the small change.

Nothing of interest occurred through the winter; but I got absolutely sick of doing nothing, and hailed the first signs of spring with delight. I went to Buffalo again, and obtained work on a large lunatic asylum that was in course of erection.

I had only worked a few weeks on this asylum when a man with whom I had worked the previous summer came to me and said that a new railway was being built, called the Rochester and State Line, from Rochester, in New York State, to Salamanca, on the boundary between New York State and Pennsylvania.

He had a job to go to on it, and he could take a mate. I agreed to go, as I knew him, and we both preferred the country to the town. We went, and for some months things went very well.

Salamanca is on the Alleghany River, twelve miles from Alleghany village, also on the river, and about eighty miles from Buffalo. Salamanca was then (in 1873) an Indian Reservation. It is, perhaps, one yet; but some reservations have been taken from the Indians, and other lands given in exchange, and this may have shared the same fate.

This, if the reservations could be made very valuable, is, in my opinion, quite right, as the Indians would only block progress, and the United States has always compensated them.

The Alleghany River here is broad but, except in floods, very shallow. We worked on bridges at Salamanca and other parts of the line towards Rochester till autumn was approaching. It was a very fine summer, and I was rapidly getting accustomed to the United States, and thinking of settling there and taking out papers of naturalization, thus becoming a citizen.

So far what I have said about my experience in America has been one continuous record of progress. Certainly, owing to the climate, I had been idle during the winter, but that was foreseen and provided for, and in fact is to-day the normal state of affairs in the building trade in America.

But now a storm was brewing all over the States, and, like all great financial convulsions, there were no doubt plenty of premonitory symptoms to warn the keen business man, or even the average citizen who took in a daily paper. I was no business man, but a workman, single, and with no care but to find work, and that I had found; and, above all, in the little villages amongst which I was employed I never saw a daily paper, or I should have known what was taking place.

The United States, after the war was finished, had entered upon an unprecedented career of prosperity, which had lasted eight years, and was now going to be succeeded by a depression equally remarkable.

I will just mention one little incident here which might have given me a hint of the state of things if I had been a business man.

My landlord was in business, and was a very regular, punctual man—one of those whose word was his bond. Coming in one day to dinner, I remarked on the absence of the boss, as we boarders called him. The landlady said he was away trying to get some money, and mentioned incidentally that money was very bad to get. On these public works, such as railways, we were paid once a month, and a month's back time was kept. The contractors guaranteed the board money, though what was their method of dealing with slippery customers I don't know, as I never thought of sliding out of any obligations. As I was owing about a month's board, although the month was not up, I said to a young Scotchman who boarded with me that it would be a good thing to pay the landlord now, as he was short of money

The Scotchman agreed, but said he was short of the full amount. I said I could put that right, and took the opportunity that evening of putting the money in the landlord's hand.

I should not have mentioned this, but, as it turned out, it had far-reaching consequences, and a most unexpected sequel.

I shall not forget my landlord's look of surprise when I gave him the money. He thought we were dissatisfied, and were going to leave. It may be a satire on this best of worlds, but the fact is that two or three times in my life I have seen a little action like this done unexpectedly, and each time the person obliged has been for a moment the picture of astonishment.

Shortly after this we finished the bridges on the section on which we were working. The Scotchman and I had each about two months' (with our back time) wages due; but when the time came for us to be paid, there was no money.

The financial situation was already affecting the construction of this new railway. The contractor by whom we were employed was very much upset, but we knew that it was no fault of his; he was waiting to be paid as well as us. As we had paid our board, we were in no quandary about that, and the Scotchman, with whom I had been mates for some time, left, leaving his affairs in the hands of our landlord, who, being a business man on the spot, undertook to receive the Scotchman's wages when the railway company paid, and remit it to him.

My case was different. I had been for some time, as I have already stated, thinking of settling. Buffalo was a great railway centre, and my idea was to get a small farm in the country, on which I could live in the winter and work on the railways in the season.

I had gone so far as to pick out a small place, and was only waiting for the end of the season to pay so much down and leave the rest on mortgage.

I thought that the hitch about the money would only be temporary, as wages must be paid in the States as well as in England, or even a powerful corporation, like a railway company, would find itself in an awkward position.

This reasoning was perfectly just, and the very calmness with which the natives and residents awaited the time when they should receive their money helped me to buoy myself up with the idea that a few weeks, at most, would put things straight.

But, though I could foresee that the wages must be paid some time, it was beyond my powers to see how long the crisis would last. I may as well state here that, as far as I know, this was the worst crisis that has ever befallen the United States.

This was the year 1873. I can say little of the beginning of it, for, as I have expressly stated, I saw no newspapers, but the failure of Jay Cooke's bank was something that even dwarfed the failure of the Glasgow bank, which took place two or three years later, in Scotland.

I have passed through some queer times since, and have seen streets standing empty here in England, but the people seemed calm, and accustomed to poverty, whilst in the States the people seemed almost paralyzed with dismay. I have heard well-to-do men say that they had letters standing on the mantelpiece fourteen days, before they could find the money to pay for a stamp, and yet they had land, houses, and plenty of credit.

It was during this terrible depression that O'Donovan Rossa, of New York, chartered steamers to bring returning emigrants from America to the Old Country. He charged fifteen dollars, whilst the regular fare was twenty-eight.

But to return to my own affairs. Thinking, as I have said, it was only a passing cloud, I drew my money out of the bank, and made a first payment for the small farm that I had chosen. With a view to keeping the interest down, I made the payment as big as I could, and looked forward to earning sufficient next season (1874) to pay the second payment.

But the winter passed, and the spring, and yet the railway did not start, nor were the wages paid till about the latter end of June, but, as I was many miles distant at the time, I am not quite sure of the date, and I had left my affairs in the hands of my landlord, who had power to let the farm also, whilst I was seeking work

CHAPTER XVII

ON TRAMP

BUT it was only on public works that there was any demand for stone-cutters, the houses in the country and in the provincial towns being of wood, and it was precisely these public works that suffered most from the depression. Failing to find work at my trade, I resolved to go and labour at anything, or anywhere that I could get it. But this was not easy to get, and I saw that I would never be able to meet the next year's payment on the farm; and then there was the interest to be paid. I sought high and low, and got some little labouring jobs, but for the most of the time a fatality seemed to dog my steps.

If I went to a job I was either just too soon or too late, and the midsummer came, and I had still never received my wages. I had made up my mind to let the farm go, but still was determined to stay in the States, and begin again from the bottom of the ladder. My landlord was staying in New York City, where he had got an appointment, but his family still lived in the country. I wrote to them, saying that the first chance I had, I would settle up for board that I was owing, and that if the State Line Company paid up whilst I was absent, they were to pay themselves out of what was coming to me.

I had got as far south as Pittsburg, and from there up the Monongahela Valley, past where the river splits up into two branches, one of which is called, I believe, the Youghioghany.

I had asked for work at a farm, and a young man said to me : " There isn't a job here, but I can tell you where you can get one, about three miles off. If you hurry up, you will catch the farmer before he goes out after dinner."

It was a very hot day, but I did hurry up, and caught the farmer, sure enough, only to be told by him that the young man had made a fool of me, and that he wanted no help.

I looked at him for a few seconds, then I asked how far off was the railway line. He said, "About three miles," and I asked in which direction. He pointed, and bidding him "Good-day," I set off at once.

During those few seconds a sudden resolution had come into my mind. I said to myself that I would never ask for another job in the country, but that I would go back to England, if I had to beg my way to New York and then work my passage home. I wanted to know where the railway was, so as to know the direction, for in these narrow Pennsylvanian valleys the road was never very far from the railway.

I have heard tell of Dame Fortune (which makes Fortune to be a female), and I remember having seen the phrase, " Fortune, fickle jade," which, if it is true, marks her as inconstant, as the rest of her sex; but at that time I had never heard what I have since been told—namely, that Fortune is a female, who, if you pursue her eagerly, will evade you, and laugh at your efforts; but if you turn your back on her with unfeigned contempt, will come and lick your boots. Only, the contempt must be unfeigned.

Five minutes before, I was an anxious individual, homeless, penniless, wondering what I would do when the autumn came, with a payment to be met, or else heavy interest to pay, and, above all, dreading to go back to the part where (with plenty of money) I had felt myself independent.

Five minutes had elapsed, and I was still homeless, but what matter? In America (at least, in the States) there is no law to punish one for sleeping on the highway. Penniless, but I could beg for food, and, if work was offered, I would take it; and as for the future, my mind was made up—I would go back and see my former landlord, pay all up (if the company had paid) and, if not, leave my claim in his hands, and also the power to hand over the farm to the person from whom I had bought it (a neighbour of his, and an old friend), and then, as soon as possible, return to Old England.

Only those who, after a long series of misfortunes, have felt that at last they have passed the worst can realize how I felt at this time. I was in the Valley of the Youghioghany, which flows into the Monongahela, which latter meets the Alleghany at Pittsburg, and at Alleghany village, twelve miles from Salamanca, almost at the head of the Alleghany River, lived the contractor for whom I had worked.

I had a clear course, if a long one, before me. The railways followed the river, and I set out for the first definite stage—namely, to Pittsburg—with a bold step; the sun above was fit to roast one, but my mind was that intent on my new plans that I never heeded it, but monotonously plodded on, knowing that at last I knew where I was going to.

Will it be believed?—I don't think I had walked an hour when, on passing a few houses not sufficient to call a village, I heard someone shouting after me. Turning round, I saw a man, who said: "Do you want a job?" My answer may be guessed, and in a few minutes I was under a roof with food before me, and work to start at in the morning.

It seems that somebody having business in Pittsburg was going to build a brick villa in this place. Now, I have said all the houses in the country were of wood, therefore a man, a brick-moulder by trade, had come and taken the job to make the bricks on the spot.

Sufficient clay had been dug and tempered, and a squad had worked vigorously, for the moulder was on piece. About two days were needed to complete the estimated quantity, when the man who worked in the clay-pit, among the clay and water with his shoes and stockings off, had stuck a pick into his big toe and was laid up. I happened to be coming past directly after, and took his place.

Two days finished the job; the moulder paid me, and I settled for my board. I meant to keep all the money for a last resource, but one of the men said: "I suppose you will be going with the train to Pittsburg; I'll go with you." I would have walked; but this man threw out a hint that the moulder, a Pittsburg man, would most likely have something more to do at Pittsburg, and that he would put in a word for me, as he liked me for a mate.

Refusing a chance of work was no part of my plans, so I agreed, and the fare to Pittsburg made a great hole in the remaining part of my two days' pay. When we got to Pittsburg, this man could not get a job for himself, much less for me; but he did not lose heart all at once, and as I had a sort of superstitious dread of refusing a chance that had so miraculously offered itself, the result was that I stayed in Pittsburg two nights, one of which was Sunday night, in what would be called here a "spike," or vagrant ward, in Du Quesne Way in Pittsburg.

This place, known as the Young Men's Home, was a place where outcasts and tramps could sleep on the bare boards, and wash themselves. There was a superintendent, and on the Sunday we were treated to a liberal allowance of Bible-reading, and allowed to pass the whole of the day inside, but on week-days we were supposed to go out and look for work. No food, if I recollect right, was given, although I may have made a slight error here, as on Sundays one could not look for work, and there was no test labour attached to the place.

But anyhow I had a little money left, and that accounts for me not being absolutely certain about this point. There were all sorts in the place, and a goodly number of English compositors and other mechanics, shoemakers and coopers mostly. Talking to them, I soon found that they all attributed their present position to drink, and would not believe a sober man could be penniless.

To do them justice, they were mostly men in their prime—sharp, active, and full of a good-natured, reckless generosity, offering to put me on to where one was sure to get food (but they used a slang term), if he would face the rapper.

Towards the evening of the Sunday I got into an awful state. I bitterly regretted breaking my new-made resolution never to ask for work, although in this case it was the fault of the man who had made (I believe out of pure kindness) a sort of half-promise.

I now understood why tramps took the denial of work so calmly, simply moving on to try somewhere else. The movement in the open air takes a lot off the mind. I said to myself if I were outside never more would I listen to anyone, but take the path I had traced out; but soon I began to think I would never get out alive.

Physiology is a subject on which I am very weak, as any attempt at reading it up makes me shudder. This may be weakness, but it is a fact. Besides having, as a rule, excellent health, I have never needed to study it.

Therefore, if what I am going to relate seems not very probable, I can only say it is the naked truth. I thought on my position, and worked myself up till the blood oozed (not gushed, as one reads often) out of my nostrils, and I felt as if it was oozing out of my ears. The room seemed to be full of fog, or I was becoming blind.

A man said to me: "Are you ill?" I said: "I am that ill that I cannot see you, although I can hear your voice." I managed to resign myself to the worst, and not complain, when my attention was attracted, by one word, uttered by a man who was in conversation with another man, though I could see neither of them.

This one word was the name of a village near Alleghany, a village where I had worked. Turning to the man who had just spoken, I said: "Have you been at —— "

"Yes, I have just come from there."

"Have the men been paid their wages yet?"

"Yes."

"Are you quite sure?"

"Yes,"—he was certain. I felt much better already, and laying myself down on the boards, I resigned myself for the night, and looked forward to the morning.

When it came I left as soon as possible, and walked twenty miles that day. As I followed the railway track up the Alleghany Valley I could count the mile-posts.

Let me state here that at that time there was no punishment for walking on the line in the States, and perhaps there is none yet. I thought that I had done very well for the first day, and felt I would soon be all right again. I crept into a little hut by the side of the line and, as it rained that night, was quite warm.

If this seem strange, it is true; if the nights were fine, they turned almost frosty towards the break of day, and a cold, icy dew fell that was dangerous, as I heard, and as I once experienced. Next day, and the rest of the days, I rose at dawn, and did a good stretch before the sun got too hot. In the heat of the day I rested, and resumed my journey towards the evening.

As long as my money lasted I bought some bread, and slept out every night where I could get shelter. In this manner I came through Kitanning, where there was a beautiful bend in the river, through Warren, and Franklin, right up the Alleghany River, till finally I came to Salamanca and Alleghany village.

I found that my landlord was still in New York City, but I got a few dollars that remained after I had paid all my accounts, and left for Buffalo. I was owing some money there, and after paying it all up and resting a few days, I left again for New York, intending to come to England that way in order to have a final interview with my landlord. I had speculated and lost, but I was already regarding the fact as a blessing in disguise, seeing that it was the cause of my return to the Old Country. I had only a few cents when I left Buffalo, but I was determined to beat my way through.

For certain reasons I came a roundabout way first, by what was called the Buffalo, New York, and Philadelphia route. This led me through by Franklinville and Alleghany, a route that I was somewhat acquainted with. I followed the roads till I came to Franklinville, and I think it was at this village—at least it was a village just before coming to Alleghany (the villages there were scattered)—that I had a rather strange experience.

I had slept out, I think, two nights, and it was towards the evening of a Saturday that I found myself on the outskirts of Franklinville.

I stopped before a house that stood by itself and was hidden from the village by a bit of rising ground. The house was in good condition, and well fenced in from the road. A man and woman stood before the house; the man had been sweeping the roadside in front of the house for the week-end, and his attitude, bending over the broom, prevented me from seeing his face.

One thing struck me: the man had swept the dust so that it formed a sort of raised footpath across the road, and it was exactly at the end of this footpath that the woman stood. I asked the time, and one or two questions about the road, which the woman answered, and, whilst speaking, she kept looking at her feet and kicking the dust up, whilst the man still leant over the broom-handle.

Presently, without looking up, the man said something to the woman about disturbing the dust after he had swept it together. She replied in a manner that annoyed the man more, and he spoke rather sharply. As I thought they were going to argue about it, and the question did not concern me at all, I went on my way.

I have just said that the house was hidden from the village by rising ground, up which my way led. This rising ground, and the fact that I had been walking all day, and now felt weary, made my pace somewhat slow, which, perhaps, was providential.

Anyhow, I had not got far up the bank when I heard someone shouting, in that tone that arrests attention at once.

Looking round towards the house, the man and woman had disappeared from view, but there was a girl, apparently about fourteen, who was jumping and waving her hands, and shouting: "Come back! for God's sake come back!" I went back, and as soon as the girl saw that I was fairly coming back, she bolted off the nearest way to the village, and I saw her no more. I could still see neither the man nor the woman, but I was certain that the trouble was with them, and when

I got in front of the house, and could see past the corner, there they were.

The man had the woman by the throat with the left hand, and had an American axe in his right, with which he was trying to strike her, but he was too close, and had too long a hold of the handle to succeed all at once, and the woman was keeping him off as well as she could, with both her hands. Still, she was bleeding, and the man was evidently a good deal the strongest, and would soon overpower her. They were in their own grounds, with a good post-and-rail fence between me and them.

The woman was looking towards me, and the man had his back to me, so that I had still not seen his face. I am anything but a giant, and had no weapon, while the man was both bigger and had an American axe (weapon enough) in his hand.

All this flashed through my mind, but saying to myself that I was only a tramp, what was my life worth ? I got over the fence, and going up to them, I said quite calmly : " What is the matter ?"

The man turned round, and I saw his face. Looking at me, he shouted: "Here's God Almighty sent a man across the Atlantic to save your life. Then, addressing himself to me : " Hold her until I get a summons for her," and went on incoherently. I said : " Certainly, get one at once, and I'll see that she does not get away in the meantime."

Off he bolted, to my great satisfaction, and the woman was endeavouring to tell how it happened, but she could scarcely speak. There was, however, no need for her to exert herself, for a man soon appeared, followed by another, and others, till there was a small crowd, for the girl had raised the village.

These men told me that the man had already been in a lunatic asylum. I have spoken about his face; it resembled that of a very old child, round, flat, and wrinkled. I had need of all my self-control to prevent my disgust being seen when he was speaking to me.

After explanations, I told the men I must go on my way, but I said the man should be put away again as soon as possible. A sister of the woman was standing on the doorstep (the woman herself had gone inside). The sister, after asking me a few questions, said: "Then you will be on tramp?"

"Yes."

"Then you had better be going again." I went.

CHAPTER XVIII

LIFE ON THE ROAD

As if to show how much stranger truth is than fiction, before the night passed I was to go through an adventure which, for a time, almost rendered me helpless with fear, and yet perhaps I was never in any danger, whilst during the time the lunatic faced me with the axe I was perfectly calm.

It came about like this : The summer was now well advanced, and a lot of hay was cut.

Now, at the time of which I write I never saw a haystack in America ; hay was all put in barns, and I had already learnt that the smell of the new hay was disliked by the mosquitoes. Therefore, when I saw a barn by the roadside, with a lot of new hay in it, I said to myself : " The very thing for a good night's rest." The barn was in two stories, in one part, and the hay was packed, so that I could get easily on to the upper part. I slipped in and got on the highest part without asking leave.

This was a mistake, but it was never repeated by me. I lay down, and after a time I heard someone come and shut the barn up for the night. I lay thinking how lucky I was, with a good night's rest before me, and no mosquitoes to fear. It was very soon dark, and I was just beginning to fall into a doze, when I heard a door open in the side of the barn, opposite to the side facing the road, and in bounced a big dog. I could see nothing, but I could tell he was big by his snorting breathing, and I could hear him clambering up the hay to where I was, and now and then slipping back on the hay.

I was now wide awake, and thoroughly frightened. Courage is a grand thing, but it is robbed of half its glory if it is accompanied by ignorance of the real danger. I was absolutely without a weapon (I never carried a knife even as a boy), and I knew if I was tackled by the dog, in the struggle we might both fall to the bottom, and though the hay would soften the fall, yet I might fall undermost, in which case I would be at a disadvantage.

I had plenty of time to let all this pass through my mind, for the dog kept slipping on the hay as he was climbing up, but I could hear he was gradually gaining, though he never made a bark, for his breathing was becoming horribly distinct.

I was lying on my right side, and I placed my left arm across my neck, so that he could not seize my throat, and I determined if he bit me to seize him by the throat and strangle him.

The position in which I had placed my arm left my left cheek exposed, and those who know more about dogs than I do may smile, but I am relating the exact truth when I say that the dog, having finally reached the top, came towards me as if he could see perfectly, and just touched my cheek with his nose, and then immediately wheeled round and went to the bottom again like a flash.

I heard the door slam again, and I once more resigned myself to sleep, thankful that I had kept perfectly still.

" No more going into barns without asking leave," I said to myself. Twice more before I reached New York I had encounters with dogs (one of them a rather strange one), yet I never thought of carrying a stick.

When I woke it was daylight, and Sunday morning. I got outside as soon as possible, and passed through Alleghany village.

I was now approaching the pass by which the railway went over the Alleghany Mountains, but I did not reach it that day. I slept that night on the step of a school. Next day I saw that I was nearing the pass. The valley narrowed, and the hills, covered with pine-trees, closed in on the road more and more. There seemed to be a good deal of wood-cutting going on, and I could hear circular saws with their vicious hum on all sides. At last I got fairly on to the railway, and began to mount the hills.

When I came to the summit, there was a long and heavy freight train standing on the line. I fell into conversation with a young man who was a brakesman on this train.

He was a Manxman, and when he found I was

from England he said I could have a ride down to Emporium (I think this was the name), about seven miles down the mountains. As the line was a single track, the freight train had to stand at certain places.

At last we got the signal to start, and once fairly set going we began to whiz down the zigzags, all the brakes locked as tightly as possible. The Manxman was kept busy tightening the brakes and running along the top of the train.

About half-way down I saw a solitary brick building on the right hand and at some distance from the line, to which it was connected by a short siding. I asked my companion what that building was, and he said it was an engine-house, where a huge engine was kept, and when trains ascended the zigzags (we were coming down) this engine came behind them and aided them.

The scene was wild and impressive. Presently our train stood still for a long interval, which was utilized by the driver to give himself a most elaborate wash and dress up (on the engine, be it understood). After giving the most minute care to his moustache and hair, he set the train in motion, and we steamed easily into Emporium, where the driver gave his hat a final jaunty set, stepped off his engine, and went his way as if he had just set out after breakfast to an office.

I have many times since, when seeing the grimy engine-drivers in England, thought what a liar they would put me down for if I told them what

I saw on the Buffalo, New York, and Philadelphia in 1874.

As I had (thanks to the Manx brakesman) got on further than I expected that day, I pursued my way eastward on the line that we had struck as far as a place called Waverly, where someone allowed me to sleep in an outhouse that night.

Next morning I set out, sometimes on the railway and sometimes on the road. It had rained during the night, and I passed over a stream that was rushing down into the main valley. The bridge was a rustic, shaky-looking affair, and I said to a man who was working by the roadside: "What is the name of this stream?" He straightened himself up, and said emphatically: "The Driftwood branch of the Sinnamahone." (I spell this name as I think best, as I have never seen it in print.)

I got on to the buffers of a freight train, and managed to ride as far as Driftwood. I shall remember Driftwood. It was in a narrow valley through which a river—the Susquehanna, I think —flows, and the hills close in so on the narrow valley that one has to look up to see their tops.

I managed to get something to eat, and when it got dark I stole on to another train, and, after a lot of dodging, I lay down on a shallow, open truck laden with small coal. I fell asleep on the coals, and was awakened by a thunder-shower which fairly made the small coals run, so that I was like going head first down between the buffers, but managed to draw myself up again.

When I got as far as Harrisburg I determined to change my route, and I walked up a line that came from Elmira to Harrisburg. I followed up the side of a stream that came down a narrow valley, walking all the way and sleeping wherever I could.

At last the line began to ascend rapidly at the head of this valley, and the stream resolved into one or two little rills. I contrived to steal a ride on the buffers of a freight train, but for the first time I got a proper chill.

When we got to Elmira, a warm-hearted Irishman paid for two big cups of hot coffee that put a little heat in my frame, but it was noon before I felt anything like warm. I was now on the Erie line, and I determined to keep near it for the remainder of my journey to New York.

Coming to a place called Binghampton, I was astonished to see a splendid stone building, standing on a gentle slope facing the south and looking as if it was a piece of Old England, so park-like was the grass, that had been just cut and was lying spread over the ground.

While I was admiring this building, I became aware of the presence of a man, who was seated on some rails at the side of the road. I found he was an Englishman, and, like myself, on the road, but not bound for any place in particular.

He informed me that the building was an inebriate asylum, and that the patients were all swells with any amount of money. He said: "Let us go and ask for a job to make this hay.

I know we won't get one, for there is a lot of assistants who have nothing to do hardly; but it will be an introduction, and we can ask for something to eat." I agreed, and we went up to the house.

The governor, who was one of the most striking-looking men I have ever seen, was in an office. We asked for a job to make the hay. He replied that they had plenty of hands belonging to the place, whereupon we put in our reserve card. We were sorry, work was hard to get, could we have a bite, as we were hungry and disappointed?

A smile of intelligence passed over his face, but he said: " Well, get along there." We went into the kitchen, passing under arches till I thought myself in some old-world monastery. The servants poured out a huge cup of tea for each of us.

It was long since I had any, and I was that eager to drink some that I put in a spoonful of salt that I thought was crystallized sugar. The servants laughed, and I soon had another cup. Coming out, I bade farewell to my English acquaintance, and went on my road.

I have said that I had two other affairs with dogs before I reached New York, and it was somewhere about here that one of them occurred.

I was walking along the road, which was simply soft sand with a worm fence of timber at the sides, when something, I know not what (was it instinct?), caused me to turn round suddenly. I had seen nothing nor heard any sound, but when I turned round, there was a big yellow dog following close to my heels, and with his nose almost touching my right hand, which I was swinging as I walked.

When I turned round he stopped, but never made a sound, and after looking at him an instant, I turned again and went on, but my mind was full of thoughts about him. There were no houses in sight. Where did he come from? What did he mean by following me like a shadow?

Perhaps he was mad; but though he looked surly, he didn't strike me as being mad. I worked my right hand as far as possible up my coat-sleeve, and kept walking on. At last I saw a small house, not at the roadside, but apparently at the end of the road. Coming nearer, I saw that the road I was on diverged at an acute angle from its present direction, and that another road joined it like a Y, and the cottage was so placed between the roads that it was directly facing me.

My mind was immediately made up. The left-hand branch of the road was on slightly lower ground than the other one. The dog was keeping his nose as if he was watching to seize my right hand. As soon as I came to the fork of the road I made a couple of steps as if I was going to take the left branch. As I expected, the dog immediately changed his direction; then, wheeling suddenly to the right, I was directly in front of the cottage, and, being on the high side of the road, I was ready to keep him at bay with my feet till some-one came out.

When I wheeled, the dog set up his bristles,

and made a grab at my hand, but with the two turns he was out of his reckoning, and, as I have seen once or twice since, having missed his aim, he did not try twice. He went into the garden at the back of the house: whether he belonged there or not I don't know. No one came out of the house, and I went on my way.

CHAPTER XIX

NEW YORK

IN travelling by the road, I sometimes had to cross bridges, and there was a bridge not far from this place, where a toll had to be paid. I used to ask my way a good distance ahead, and I had been told of this bridge. I was now in that state of mind that I just relied on things turning up at the last moment, and, though I had no money, I went straight on.

This particular bridge, I believe, was over the Delaware River, which is very small here. I had slept outside, and woke up early. The morning was cool, but promised a hot day. The smell of new-mown grass was in the air, and I felt cheerful—in fact, more cheerful than many who had homes. The way I was pursuing was very narrow, and a lot of bramble-berries grew by the side. I was eating some of these, when I heard a horse coming at a gentle pace.

Looking up, I saw a waggon, like those used in England to haul timber; that is to say, a pair of wheels in front and a pair behind, with a long pole connecting them. Two long thin planks were laid on this frame, and there was a small bundle of grass and a tarpaulin at the hind end of the waggon. On the front were seated two men; one (evidently a teamster) was driving, and the other was very well dressed, and appeared to be riding for pleasure.

I asked for a lift. The driver said: "Jump on," and I did. I said: "How far are you going?" and the driver replied that they were going to bring in some hay that they had cut. He whipped up the horse, and we proceeded at a gentle trot. After going, I think, about two miles, I thought it was a long distance to fetch hay from the fields. Then the tarpaulin began to slip off with the jolting. Thinking it was as little as I could do for my ride, I took hold of the tarpaulin, and began to haul it in, and stow it properly.

In doing so, I became aware of a black valise, silver-mounted, which the slipping of the tarpaulin had uncovered. I covered it again at once. Then the two men started to talk in whispers, and I heard the driver say: "He's all right; he is only a tramp." Then the driver started to question me, but every answer I gave confirmed his view that I was all right, and the two continued their whispered conversation. Thus we went for miles, till, at last, the driver pulled up at the side of the road, and the other man jumped off, the driver handed him the valise, and told me he was not going any farther. I jumped off too.

After the waggon had gone back, the stranger turned to me and said: "There is a bridge near here. If you will carry my valise over the bridge

I will pay your toll, and stand you a drink at the other side."

This, when I was wondering how I could get over, was just a specimen of what takes place every day in real life. He went on to state that he had got into a row the night before, and was frightened of being arrested as a fugitive if he carried the valise, but, once over the bridge, he was in another county (or, at least, in another jurisdiction).

I forget the name of the place, but I carried the valise over, and we had a drink, and bade each other "Good-bye." I was now sure that I had got my task under hand. I can only remember sleeping one night in the open air after crossing this bridge, but one evening, about six, I came on to a farm, and saw a man sitting milking a cow.

I asked him if I could sleep in his barn. He said: "Would you not be better sleeping in a good bed?"

"Very likely, but I am quite content with a barn." He insisted on me having supper, and sleeping in the house. He wanted me to stay and have breakfast, but, thanking him, I was off as usual in the cool of the morning.

The next evening I had a rather peculiar experience. I found a freight train standing, and, looking along it, I saw a car laden with planks or battens. These battens were all of one size, and this size was about two and a half feet shorter than the length of the car. At the time I sighted the car the battens were all lying with their ends resting against the forward end of the car.

This left an open space, like a pit, about two feet six inches broad at the end of the car, and about three feet six inches high; the length of this pit, of course, was the width of the car. I said to myself: "This is a chance," and got into the car, and down into this pit.

I soon felt sleepy, and was beginning to doze off, when the train started. Providence once more saved me from the effects of my thoughtlessness. If I had fallen sound asleep I would never have got out of the car alive, for the car commenced to mount up a steep grade (the railways in America were not as level as here), and, of course, the battens commenced to slide back to the end where I was lying.

I was roused by the pressure, and, looking up, I saw the battens sliding. I sprang to my feet like lightning, and clambered on to the top of the battens just in time. The car was built like those we have here for carrying cattle—that is, the sides did not come up to the roof, but left an open space for light and air. It was through this space that I entered the car.

I now lay on the top of the battens, which reached up to this open space.

After being shunted about, and sometimes standing at sidings, we reached a small village. It was Sunday morning, and daylight. I got out of the car in a hurry. When I dropped on the ground my feet went out below me, and I fell on my back in a puddle. My legs were cramped with cold, but I got up and walked on to restore the circulation.

I saw a sort of hand-barrow by the side of the railway, and as it was Sunday I concluded no one would need it that day. It was better than the damp ground, and, as I had not slept in the car, I lay down on it and fell sound asleep.

I was awakened by the voices of people passing to church. "Poor fellow!" I heard some women say. But though I had about sixty miles to go, yet I had done my last tramp, for on speaking to a few of the natives, they told me that a milk-train went into the city in the evening, and that I could most likely get a lift in with it. I have no recollection of how it was done, but I managed to get on to this train.

It was night, and the only part of which I have any idea was the tunnels. Lying on an open truck, I could see the rough, naked surface of the rock above me. Nor have I any memory of how the tunnel was lit up, but the flickering glare on the rock above me dwells in my mind. I was now coming to the celebrated city for the first time, penniless and with only the hope of borrowing my passage money to England from a Yankee.

New York proper is on an island, and I think it would be Jersey City at which the line I had come by (the Erie) terminated. The train ran on to a wharf built of wood, and I was looking for a place to lie down till daylight when a man came up to me with a bull's-eye lantern, and turned the light right in my face.

"What are you doing?"

"I am looking for a place to lie down."

"Where do you come from?"

I told him briefly, and pointed to the train, saying: "I have just come on that train."

"Where are you going?"

"To England from New York."

"Well, come on, then; the ferry-boat is just going to start."

"But I have no money."

"How the devil, then, are you going to England?"

I told him that a friend of mine in New York would lend me the money.

After looking at me again, he said: "Well, come on board."

I went, and thought I was in the aisle of a great cathedral, roofed in with glass. The boat, of course, soon crossed the river, and I remained standing in the one place till we had crossed, as I had paid no money, and did not like to walk round.

At last I was in New York; it was just breaking day, and some homeless ones like myself were washing their faces at a sort of public fountain. I had a wash also, and began to look around me. The part where I had landed did not seem particularly cheerful; but I only intended putting in the time till between eight and nine, at which later hour my friend would leave for his office.

My intention was to call on him before he left, but the fates willed it otherwise.

Somehow or other I got into conversation with an Irishman, whom I told that I was going to see a gentleman in East Broadway, and asked him if he could direct me to it. He said he was out of work, and no prospects of getting it, so that his time was of no value, and that we could walk about in the meantime, and he would conduct me there in time. I have not the slightest idea of the streets or locality about which we wandered, as I simply followed my companion about; but whether it was that East Broadway was a part that he seldom visited, or whether I had slightly miscalculated the time at which my friend would leave, I shall never know, but the fact is that when I did get there and inquired my friend had gone.

This was a disappointment; there was nothing for it but to put in the weary day. I now wished myself clear of my companion; but I knew he would look for something for his trouble, and I had nothing. Had I been alone I would have found some place or other where I could have laid myself down and slept; but my companion kept remarking that New York was a funny place, and that it was as much as my life was worth to lie down. He had got into the real style of loafing the streets; for myself I would have spent the day in visiting the sights of the city, which would have passed the time, but he would hear of nothing but just sauntering back and forward.

What was the use of wearing our shoes out and

tiring and hungering ourselves? However, he stuck close to me; he evidently had nothing, and he had seen by my face, when the servant said my friend had gone, that my tale was true, and he counted on finally getting something.

The sun got hotter and hotter. How I passed that wretched day I don't know. I could not even occupy myself with my own thoughts, for I had to make some sort of answer to his remarks. However, he had persistence, for he stuck to me the whole day.

The only thing I remember seeing during that day (we never tasted food) was a man, evidently a labourer, sound asleep in the sunshine on a big iron plate. The plate was one of those that are laid on the ground to wheel bricks on.

But at last the sun gave signs of afternoon, and at last the hour approached when I knew that my friend would be at his lodging. Only those who have been compelled to remain inactive, waiting for a chance to get work or something to eat, can realize my feelings when the time came for action.

This time I took the initiative, and inquired diligently the time, and landed at the place at the proper hour. East Broadway was a wide street, and all that I can remember is that the street had a rise in one direction, so that when you looked up the gradient, the part I wanted was on the left side, and the houses had a few broad stone steps leading up to the front-doors.

I know the number, though I don't give it here. My companion stood on the pavement, while I went up the steps. Rapping at the door, a servant came.

"Is Mr. —— here?"

"Yes."

"Would you mind telling him that a man wishes to speak to him for a minute?" The servant disappeared, and my friend came to the door. He looked, and said: "Is that you?"

"Yes; what is left of me," I said. "I am going to England, and if it was land all the way I would not have troubled you, but I want you to lend me some money to go." He looked and hesitated.

"I hope you don't doubt my honesty?"

"No; but you know how I am situated, and I doubt your ability to repay me in time."

"But I am not without friends in England, and I can pay you back. I only want twenty dollars."

"But you can't go to England with twenty dollars" (the regular fare was twenty-eight).

"But," I said, "O'Donovan Rossa is chartering a steamer and taking them for fifteen. I will manage." He put his hand into his pocket, and gave me a twenty-dollar bill. I thanked him, and shook hands, and said good-bye.

Thus I left a genuine Yankee, whose striking resemblance to the portraits of Abraham Lincoln had first drawn my attention, and who had proved himself a man and a gentleman.

Let me hasten to add that I repaid him promptly; but of that more hereafter.

When I went down the steps my companion said: "You must be a queer b——."

" How so ? "

" Why, you, a tramp, to know people living in this place, and to get that money for just asking." I don't know what I said in reply; but I sought out a lodging-house. We both had something to eat. I gave my companion something, I don't know how much it was, but it couldn't be much. He seemed disinclined to leave, and wanted more.

But I pointed out to him that I, a perfect stranger, had only asked to be directed to East Broadway; that he had not taken me there in time, although we had hours before us; that he, an Old Countryman, knew the fare to England as well as I did; and that I had to live in expensive New York till a boat sailed to suit me.

What could I give ?

The truth of my words impressed him, and he went away. In America they have some good ideas, born, perhaps, of necessity. I called the landlord to me, told him that I was a stranger, and that the twenty-dollar bill he had just changed for me was all my money. I wanted to pay for my bed, and would he put the rest of my money in his safe till morning? He said yes, and I knew I was all right till the next day. I went to bed early, and slept till the first dawn, when I found myself attacked by a swarm of— well, their name, I believe, is not generally printed.

An Irishman was lying in a bed close to mine. He tossed about for some time, and at last, saying, " Jesus Christ ! what have I done to be eaten alive like this ?" he got out of bed and lay down on the floor. I looked at my bed. The top part of it was literally swarming with the pests.

However, my mind was too full to pay much attention to them, and as soon as the household was moving, I got up, had some breakfast, got my money from the landlord, and went out.

I had not much time to look about me, but I went up Broadway, and saw the celebrated Trinity Church. It did not impress me much. I thought it rather small and too regular in pattern.

As soon as possible I got among the men who were out of work, and especially amongst the Old Countrymen who were trying to get back to England. Some of them told me that there was a society, called St. George's Society, for helping Englishmen home. I went at the hour they said, and saw a very pleasant gentleman, with whom I had a long conversation. He asked me a lot of questions, which I answered freely. He said that I was somewhat mistaken as to the scope and aims of the society. I understood him to say that the Englishmen they sent home were practically all sailors. I told him what money I had, and that all I wanted was a ticket by one of the liners. I said I was willing to do a certain amount of work to make up the passage money.

After some more talk he said to me suddenly: " You don't look like a man that drinks. Then, seeing my surprise, he went on to say that practically all who came to him had spent their money in drink. The upshot of our conversation was that he should see if I could get a ticket at a reduction, as the times were so exceptional, and I said I would see him again the next day.

I went out again into the streets, looking about me. I remember seeing a great sign up on a building, "Hospital for Sunstroke Patients," and shortly after saw a sign in large letters which I will never forget. It was only two words, but they could not have been better suited to my case: "Spartan Dormitory." I thanked my stars that I had read about the Spartans, and had a good idea of the meaning of the word, used (as in this case) as an adjective. I went in and saw a clean, honest-looking woman. The place was as simply furnished as it could be; she told me that I could have a warm bath and a bed for—I am sorry I have forgotten the price, but it was evidently cost price.

I had a bath, and such a night's sleep in a clean bed as I will never forget. I made no remarks, nor asked any questions, but the place must evidently have been run by philanthropic, and yet most practical, persons. There was no suggestion of charity, but a regular scale of payments at the very lowest prices.

In taking leave of this subject, I cannot help remarking that I was astonished at seeing hardly anyone taking advantage of this admirable institution. I went back and saw the official at the office of the St. George's Society. Once more I regret not having written certain things down, so that I cannot exactly state how or what he had done for me. But this I can say: I got the twenty-dollar bill, and paid for two nights' lodging and food out of it, and yet got a ticket home by an Anchor Line steamer to Glasgow. Whether the exceptional state of affairs had for a short time lowered the rates, or whether O'Donovan Rossa's enterprise was the cause, or whether this official had made representations in my behalf, I cannot say, but on the afternoon of the third day in New York I found myself on board the Anchor liner, and no money had passed from this official to me; indeed, I had never asked for any. " Hurrah for Old England !" I said, as I sprang on board without one penny, but a ticket home, in my possession.

An incident immediately occurred that will give a slight idea of the exceptional state of affairs existing at the time of which I write. In ordinary times the great shipping lines reckoned on very few (comparatively) emigrants on the home passage, and took more freight accordingly. Thus, when my fellow-passengers rushed downstairs to stow their luggage and mattresses in their bunks, I never hurried myself.

I had no mattress and no luggage. Soon there was a commotion ; there were so many emigrants returning, that there were not sufficient bunks at liberty. What a fine illustration of the old saying, " The last shall be first, and the first last "! I, the penniless, was placed in an intermediate cabin with a cane-bottomed sleeping-bunk, as all the steerage bunks were already taken up. I pass over the passage home. The weather was fine, but we were a fortnight on the journey. We came to Greenock at eight in the morning, and took four hours to come twenty miles up the Clyde to Glasgow. I got a train in the afternoon, and after travelling all night, arrived at the station from which I had set out for America.

CHAPTER XX

I MARRY

I sought out a man whom I had known and obliged as a fellow-workman. He was now married, and a contractor. He gave me a job and a few shillings to get some tools, and I soon got some gathered together. In the course of my life I have often remarked that after a very stormy experience there comes one quite the reverse, but I have never had a more striking proof of this phenomenon than I was now having.

It was now the beginning of September; the weather was delightful, reminding me of the Indian summer of the United States. The job was a most pleasant one; we were doing some alterations to a large old mansion—modernizing it, in fact. As the weather was so fine, we worked most of the stones outside of the shed, and spread ourselves over the lawn.

The family were away during the alterations, but had left strict orders that a rookery which was close to the house was not to be disturbed. Day after day and week after week I enjoyed the delicious sunshine, and allowed my gaze to wander over the well-kept park, and watch the slight haze that was present each morning gradually disperse and be followed by a genial warmth, till the sun sank over the tops of the old trees, whose beautiful foliage, thanks to the absence of any wind, lingered till late in the autumn.

I felt myself a new man, for in addition to my beautiful surroundings I had made a new departure, and there are few things that give such a cheerful feeling as a new study or hobby. I was determined to go in for a course of mathematics.

Our lodgings were in a cottage just outside of the park gates, and within a quarter of a mile there was a mechanics' institute. The librarian and custodian was an old man, who taught arithmetic. I applied to him for lessons in algebra. The terms were reasonable—one shilling per week for five lessons; of course while the others were doing arithmetic. I made rapid progress, using Haddon's Algebra in the Weale Series.

Then I tackled the schoolboys' old friend, Euclid, then trigonometry, and the practice of logarithms. Having found these fairly easy, I tackled the calculus by myself, but here I found difficulties.

The books I used in the Weale Series were deficient in the practical illustrations, which are such a prominent feature in the modern textbooks. However, I managed to acquire sufficient mathematical knowledge to render the reading of books on mechanics or natural philosophy (this title has since almost disappeared in favour of physics) comparatively easy.

The job I was now working on lasted into the new year, and I made good use of my time through the evenings.

I paid off the money I had borrowed, and received a kind letter from my friend in America. I kept it for years, but it got lost at last. I am sorry to record that I made a great mistake in not keeping up this correspondence; but, like many others, I disliked writing letters.

The job finished up early in the year 1875, and I got another which lasted till the autumn. I still continued my studies in a desultory manner, but I was rapidly drifting into an easy-going, aimless life. The life I was leading was pleasant—too pleasant, in fact—and my experience was another proof that when a man is not going forward he is going back.

After sundry reflections on my position and prospects, and after passing a humiliating judgment on myself, I resolved to take a momentous step, perhaps the most important that a man takes—in a word, I made up my mind to get married. I was now thirty years old, and although I had saved nothing, I could not be called drunken or lazy.

Having mentioned my resolution to a few of my friends, I found that they all said about the same thing—namely, " Be very cautious," " Mind what you are doing," and so forth. I had nothing, and when I look back I cannot tell how it was. I had good wages, and certainly I never neglected work, but yet the fact was I had nothing. But I have known plenty of bachelors since, and I don't think that five per cent. of them have any more than the struggling married man.

The woman I married had as little as myself, but she was possessed of character, and principle, and but for her I am certain that, many years ago, I would have gone down in the struggle for existence.

It seems strange that a man with health, strength, and industry should have to struggle for existence, but such is the case.

To hear and read temperance speakers and writers, a man has nothing to do but be sober, and all the rest is success. I am as sober as any man except a teetotaller, and I know plenty more, and they are often without a job, whilst the boozer has jobs thrust upon him.

Of course I can give reasons for this, but I don't wish to theorize, but just state facts.

When we were married my wife and I went into a room in a friend's house for six weeks, at the end of which I took a house, and moved into it, with a few — a very few — household effects.

Shortly after, I was sitting in the house one morning, it being wet, and there was no shed on the job, when I heard a rap at the door. It was the Vicar, who lived only a short distance off. He said he always called on the new-comers as fast as the houses were taken up. I invited him in, and when he got inside he said : " Ah, I see you haven't got your furniture here yet." But he soon saw how the land lay, and we enjoyed ourselves for about an hour.

He was a graduate of Trinity College, Dublin, and he soon got hold of my books, and said he liked to see a workman try to improve his education. As he was an M.A., and made himself so free, I thought it would be a good chance to ask his opinion about some knotty points in the calculus, but, although he was quite willing, he could shed no light on it.

He said that he had so much to do that he had to confine himself to one subject of study, and that he had chosen Hebrew as his speciality. The talk then turned to the problem of all problems—namely, the problem of getting a living. He had the idea, like all his class (except, perhaps, a few of the very old clergymen), that a workman that was steady, sober, and a bit of a scholar was certain of constant employment.

I combated this view, and said that, though a foreman must be steady, and have a little scholarship, yet every workman who was sober, attentive, and given ever so slightly to books, was regarded as a possible rival by the foreman, and where the job was a small one, he was looked upon as a possible competitor by the builder himself.

I maintained then, and I am to-day of the same opinion, that the workman who liked a spree now and again, provided that he could do his work, got the best of treatment both from his fellow-workmen and from his employer. His mates all would speak of him as a good-hearted fellow, who could take a drink or let it alone, whilst his employer would smile up his sleeve, because his (the boozer's) little weakness would prevent him from starting business on his own account.

Of course, I said that my experience was only in the building trade, and that in factories, where a workman was little more than a machine-tender, things might be slightly different, as the machines must be kept going. The Vicar took his leave, but often gave me a call while I was in his district.

Things went on pretty smoothly for about two years. I gradually got some furniture scraped together, and my wife made the best and most economical use of my wages. We had one child, a boy, who, of course, was such a one as had never been seen before. I was now quite a family man. I stuck pretty well indoors at nights, and started to learn French and German. French grammars, and German also, could be picked up for a few coppers on the second-hand bookstalls. I was now in a more determined frame of mind than when I tried my hand on Lamartine in London and stuck at the word " que," and I soon managed to read both languages fairly well, though I may say *en passant* that literary German is not an easy task to read, and demands a good deal of practice, as the long complicated sentences require to be mentally analyzed in reading.

French, on the other hand, is a beautiful language to read (mentally), of course; but the pronunciation is a stumbling-block which cannot be avoided or glossed over.

As a little mental exertion is a delightful change after outdoor labour, I say things went on pretty comfortably for about two years, sometimes in work and sometimes out of work, but always enjoying my books in the evenings after the day's work was done.

But a time was coming when to be in work was an exception and to be out of work the rule.

CHAPTER XXI

LIFE'S STRUGGLES

THE wave of depression which had made itself so severely felt in the United States now seemed to have fairly laid hold of this country. Anyone who remembers the five years from 1875 to 1880 knows that the congested state of the labour market during those years could scarcely be exaggerated. A long row of houses in front of where we lived during those years were almost entirely empty, and even the staircases had been pulled down for firewood.

This was only a typical example of what was to be seen in all the towns. Everywhere crowds of men were either looking for employment or standing talking about the state of the country. As a workman put it, at one time if two men met they said, "Are you working?" but now they say, "How long have you been out?" for they know that you are not working.

For a considerable time I managed to keep my head above water, being most ably seconded and helped by my wife. But I was now rapidly learning the difference between a single and a married man—a difference which is most plainly seen and felt in times of depression.

A single man, even if he is out of work, can, if his character is good, get credit for a few weeks, and, in some cases, months at his lodgings. Finally, when he gets work, he can soon pay up his arrears. Also he can tramp to look for work, and even if he has to tramp for weeks, he has excitement and novelty.

But the married man cannot run away from his trouble. And then there is the rent. This must be paid, or else——

To-day, when I read the halfpenny evening paper, with its news columns giving the results of a far-reaching system of news agencies, if I see the paragraph heading, " Dreadful Tragedy at ——," I am thankful that I came through those years without losing my reason, and, though I can honestly say I never turned my back on work, doubly thankful that my own exertions were aided, and in some points even surpassed, by those of my wife.

I could fill volumes with the strange shifts, pinches, and expedients which we went through, some of them almost comical, but most of them bitter, and some of them all but tragical, till the tide turned, but I will only mention the principal incidents.

I had been employed fairly well for a bit, when I fell out of a job, and walked about for nearly twelve weeks. At the end of that time I removed across the street into one of the row of houses that I have spoken of that were standing empty. The rent was reduced to half a crown a week, and I got a job that lasted a couple of months. We had a second son born, and I struggled hard to get work. I managed to procure some little jobs, but as soon as I got work every shilling was swallowed up to pay debts.

For a time we appeared to be holding our own, but our clothes were wearing out, and instead of being able to get more, it was with the utmost difficulty that we could procure food. The rent went back, but as the property was in such a state we were not pressed for arrears. Countless pages have been written about poverty, but the sentence in the Old Book, " The destruction of the poor is their poverty," contains the pith of the matter.

I found that there was always some work to be had; but at what price ? Builders, when asked for work, said: " So-and-so has offered to do the job for so much." Men who could not find a job actually commenced building on nothing. They got someone who lent them money to pay wages; they got bricks, stones—in a word, material—on credit; and when the crash came, they had as much, or more, than when they started. One joiner whom I knew could not get a job started in this manner and failed for £14,000.

I took a labouring job in a factory. I was always on the night shift, Sunday night as well, Saturday night being the only night off. The hours were from five in the evening till six in the morning—thirteen hours—making seventy-eight per week, for a guinea a week, or three and sixpence per shift.

Would it be believed?—I was absolutely hated by the rest of the labourers for not belonging to their class. The job involved some writing and accounts, or I would not have got it. At the end of six weeks my health broke down, as I could not sleep through the day. I thought this a hardship at the time, but I think differently now, and call it Providence.

I soon recovered in the open air and sun, and got one or two little jobs. My wife did a little sewing, and one or two workmen came to me in the evenings for lessons in arithmetic. One fellow who had a good job, and knew how I was situated, came for lessons at sixpence per week, and forgot to turn up on Friday night, when the sixpence was due. However, he will turn up again farther on. He was a very old acquaintance, and I said nothing the next week when he came again, and I can afford to laugh now after the incident in which he will figure in due time.

As usual, I found some real diamonds in the rough amongst my fellow-workmen, but they had enough to do to provide for their own. One man whom I knew gave a lecture on phrenology, and offered me eighteenpence to take the money at the door. I only took one and ninepence altogether, although I took a lot of tickets which must have been paid for, because when we settled up after the lecture, we spent the odd threepence in a coffee-shop, and the lecturer seemed quite satisfied.

About this time the craze for spelling-bees was at its height, and a friend of mine meeting me in the street, said : " There is going to be a spelling-bee on to-night, entrance fee sixpence; I will enter you, and I think you can win." I went, but did not win. However, I got third prize, a half-crown, and welcome it was when I took it home.

They say poverty makes us acquainted with strange bed-fellows. I certainly had some strange experiences. Many people have laughed at school-boys' answers at examinations—" howlers " they are called ; but the following, I think, deserves to be preserved as a specimen of what pedagogues can do.

I got to know a schoolmaster who had a private school, but it was going down sadly under the influence of the Board Schools. Poor fellow! he thought it was the depression in trade that was doing it.

He came to me one night, and said that there was going to be an examination in music at —— in a fortnight. He knew a little about tonic sol-fa, and if I would help him with the old notation, he thought he could pass, and the certificate would perhaps draw more pupils.

I thought the train fare and the entrance fee would be money thrown away which he could ill afford, but I said I would do what I could for him. The night before the examination we were busy in view of the approaching ordeal. After asking some questions about what was likely to be on the examination paper, he said suddenly: " Do you think I should put a bit of mensuration in it ?" I looked at him and said : " What in the world would you put mensuration in it for ?" " To let them see I know something about it."

Well, he went, sat the exam., and one of the questions on the paper was : " In what scale do intervals greater than a tone occur ?" His answer was : " In the chromatic scale." If anyone should doubt this, I repeat it is absolutely true.

Having sold all my books, I became acquainted with a second-hand bookseller, who had bought them. He sometimes gave me a job to help him on the Saturday nights, which secured a little food for the Sunday. He did not pretend to know much of the inside of books, but said he was there to sell them.

One day a man who was watching the stall whilst the owner was absent bought a book from a woman for threepence. Neither this man nor the owner of the stall could make anything of this book, which was published, I believe, at two guineas. I happened to pass by at the time, and they showed me the book. I gave a glance at the book ; it was a table of logarithms by Oliver Byrne of Dual Arithmetic fame. It was a large, thin book more like a piece of music than anything else when shut. The logarithms were all contained on, I think, ten sheets, each sheet having a little flap like a pocket-book, and a number on each of these flaps.

To stiffen the book there were some pages of
mathematical formulæ. I asked the bookseller if
he would be content with three and sixpence, and
on his saying " Yes," I took it to a literary institute, and sold it to the librarian for seven shillings
and sixpence. The four shillings thus gained was
a godsend.

I used to go round seeking work in the fore-
noons, and, if I was unsuccessful, I tried all these
little schemes and dodges to earn a trifle in the
afternoons and evenings. Sometimes I managed
to secure a few days' work, and then the arrears
of rent were reduced a little.

My wife strove with almost superhuman forti-
tude to keep our two little boys respectable in
appearance. The neighbours used to say, " Nobody would think you are hard up, to look at
your children." She taught our eldest boy to
read, as we could not pay for his schooling, and
it was a solace to her when she found that he
could read fluently. I forget the name of the book
she used, but there was one piece in it which
contained these lines :

> " The gallant Crozier, and the brave Fitz James,
>   And even the stout Sir John."

In the evenings, while she mended and cleaned
their clothes, he would read aloud some of these
pieces, whilst our youngest one sat on my knee.

A woman with a large working family was ill
(but nothing serious). I had formerly lodged
with this family, and we had always kept up their

acquaintance. They had constant work, as the head of the family had been hurt in the employment of a big company, who now employed her sons.

She offered my wife ten shillings to come every morning for a week and look after her. I went in the evenings to carry our youngest one home. The woman was kindness itself to our two boys, and saw that they were well fed. I believe she thought that I was a bit lazy, but I forgive her for it, as I find there are many well-meaning people who are apt to think a man is lazy if he is much out of work. The ten shillings paid a fortnight's rent, and left us a little to get food with.

My wife was highly respected by our neighbours, some of whom said that they would trust her with anything, but they didn't care about her man; they didn't think he wanted work. Some even went so far as to counsel her to leave me altogether, saying that I would just bring her and the two boys to the workhouse. Some went farther than that, but I knew my own mind, and let it all slide, being borne up by the knowledge that I never shirked work, and forgetting some of the things that were said against me, for the sake of kindness shown to my two little ones by the speakers. One woman, a neighbour, once came into our house while I was absent, and, pulling out something nice to eat (I forget what it was), said to my wife: " Here, eat that! and I am going to stop and see that your lazy man doesn't get a bite of it."

CHAPTER XXII

OUT OF THE DEPTHS

BUT if some of poverty's experiences were almost laughable, there were others that were sad enough, and bordered upon tragedy. I know few things worse to bear than to come home, night after night, and see your young children's mute gaze, as you sit down, saying nothing, because you have brought nothing, and have no prospects. The subject is too awful to dwell upon.

One experience that I had is fixed in my memory. I had seen a small contractor two or three times about a little work that he had to do. I felt almost certain that I would get it, and had expressed myself to that effect. But, for some reason or other, he hung back, and when I came home and told my wife that I had not got a start, she became hysterical. With the utmost difficulty, I at last succeeded in getting her slightly calmed down. I went back to the contractor. I don't know what I said, but it was arranged for me to start in the morning. I took something with me for breakfast, but when dinner-time came I worked on, as the job was only a small one, and I was doing it in the contractor's own yard.

About two o'clock a woman came out of the house: I think it was the man's wife, but I am not sure. She said: "You never stopped for dinner." I replied that I had no dinner to go to. She made no answer, but went inside, and shortly after a servant came out with a good dinner on a plate. She carried it into a washhouse, and then came and told me that the mistress had sent it out for me.

This was an act of kindness, but when I finished the job I had the utmost difficulty in getting my money. The man had a very queer name, and I found him as queer as his name. At last, with a little diplomacy, I managed to get it.

I got another small job, and my wife mended the soles of my shoes every night with a one-pronged fork and twine, till Saturday came, and I bought a pair of working boots.

A man that I knew well leased a part of a quarry; that is, there were two different parties, who had taken each one end of the quarry. This man had a contract to supply a lot of stone. He had two men employed, and his own lad. He kindly offered me a share of the work, adding that the price was very low. I thanked him, and said I could earn wages if anyone else could. I started, and found that I could earn my money, but the rub was to be kept going with stone.

We were all waiting for the quarrymen, and I fell into conversation with an old man, that I had noticed was very weak, and did not appear to be earning over sixpence per day. His story was a sad one: he had been in a good position, had made a poor use of his time, finally he had got a leg broken, and, after six months' illness, was trying to earn a little to give to some of his family, who were keeping him. He said the young fellows expected him to take his turn at lifting, as if he was all right. Three shillings and sixpence was all that he had earned the previous week. I told him that I would take his turn at the lifting. Poor fellow! I only did it one day; the next I saw him leaning over his "banker." I kept my eye on him. He swerved, and fell. We got him sent home, but he was dead before he reached it. During the height of the good times he had employed the very men who were now treating him as a nuisance!

After having tried in vain to get work for a long time, I went away on tramp to seek work. I was unsuccessful, but I had one experience which I will relate here.

I came to a town where there lived one of those who used to be called merchant princes. The name is somewhat out of date; millionaires or multi-millionaires take their place now. He was a large manufacturer, and dominated the town and the local district. He was an M.P., and his name was often quoted by well-meaning but not too acute people as a great philanthropist. It was the first time I had ever been in the town, but I had often heard of him and his firm. In fact, not to have heard of him would have been rather difficult. His name was often blazoned in the Press, especially when he aired his pet question in the House of Commons. This question, in a lot of people's eyes, made him a great reformer; regeneration would hardly overstate their views of him. My own views of this question, and his particular handling of it, may be worth nothing; but time has proved them correct, for he made nothing of it.

Two men told me in this town that the great man had a place where anyone could get work, a sort of test labour institution. Of course the work was not constant; that was understood. I will give my plain, unvarnished statement of my experience, the first and last of a so-called philanthropy.

I went to the office-door promptly at one o'clock in the afternoon. Someone told me at the door that the labour-master, or whatever his title was, had not yet come back from dinner. After I had been waiting more than twenty minutes (there was a clock in the office) a man came, looked sharply at me, and asked my business. I told him. He got a great book, and asked my name and address. I gave a name and address, not my own, but one that I could verify. Then, leaning back in his chair, he asked a string of questions, and talked about everything but what I wanted. At last I told him that it was two o'clock, and I wanted to be earning something. (Significant fact, there was no one but myself seeking work.)

He jumped up, opened a door leading into a yard, and brought some lengths—say a foot long—

of old creosoted railway sleepers. Giving me an axe, he said they paid one halfpenny each for splitting these lengths into firewood. I started. I was already out of temper at the way he (who was well paid) had wasted my time. I was told to split them up on the floor of a passage which led into the back-yard of the house.

I found it an awkward job. I think he must have picked out all the knotty, twisted pieces that he could find. I worked as hard as I could, but I soon began to doubt whether I would be able to earn the fourpence necessary to pay my night's lodging. The reader will think this incredible; but if I had to do it regularly, I have no doubt that by arranging a stand for the pieces of wood I could soon split them as quick as anyone else.

However, by asking the time at intervals, I saw that I would not (at the rate at which I was progressing) be finished with eight lengths— fourpence—at five o'clock.

I thought of the humbug of paying rent, rates, etc., besides a man's wages, to watch me earning a penny an hour. Had I been the least bit of a loafer, I would have given it up after splitting one length; but I was determined to see it through, and give it a fair trial. The principal difficulty was to get the piece of wood to stand on its end, so as to split it with a blow of the axe.

But another thing was to try my temper, and put me in a frame of mind that the reader may think perhaps bordering on madness, but I will state it. When the piece of wood had been split two or three times, it, of course, became narrow and more difficult to stand on its end. Repeatedly it would fall just as I was going to strike a blow, and I would raise it again only to see it fall another time or two. As for holding it with the left hand, it was too knotty, and required a blow to split it that made holding it dangerous.

And now that last straw that always comes in to drive anyone who is worried to extremities made its appearance. I have said that I was told to split them in a passage, and at the time I thought that the yard would have been the best place. Well, shortly after I had got fairly into work I became aware of the presence of a boy about three years old. He was a fine, healthy boy, blue-eyed, with long yellow ringlets, and full (too full for me) of life. I think he must have been the son of the labour-master. Just when I raised the axe and was poising it for a blow, he would rush forward, and either the piece of wood fell from the vibration or else I was afraid to strike lest the blow should fall upon his head. At first I spoke to him, and told him to keep out of the way; but he was a spoiled darling, and took no notice.

Many a time the thought came into my head to strike, and let him take his chance (for I was maddened with the humbug of the caretaker), but I put it down, and shoved him out of the way. At last, about half-past four, the official came again, and said: "It's no use giving you another length, for you can't split it by five o'clock." He paid me the threepence due to me for splitting six lengths, and I staggered into the open air like a man drunk. This was philanthropy. The afternoon of four hours reduced to two and a half, and myself earning one penny less than I must pay for my bed that night !

After four weeks' wandering I came home to find my two boys all right, and everything in order, thanks to my wife's heroic exertions.

One thing I almost forgot to mention : the great man, the autocrat of the district, the philanthropist, what became of him ? The answer is contained in the sentence : " Let he that thinketh he standeth, take heed lest he fall." After coming home I had again a long spell of poverty, broken by some jobs now and then. But a blow quite different from any that I had yet felt was to fall on me.

Our youngest boy was a singularly handsome child, with large dark brown eyes, and hair of that peculiar shade called auburn. We had never had a photograph taken of our children, but having made up our minds to have our youngest photographed, we left the house one Saturday afternoon for that purpose.

It was a cold, dreary day in spring, with a keen east wind and leaden sky. My wife was carrying the boy, and he did not seem to enjoy the walk as usual. As he was generally very quiet, we did not notice him for a time, but at last his stillness attracted our attention. We resolved to wait for finer weather, and then have him taken in a more cheerful mood. Had we had the slightest idea of what was coming, we would have carried out our intention no matter what weather it was, and secured a portrait of him.

As it was, a few days showed that something was the matter with him; but knowing his mother's nursing powers, I did not feel at all uneasy; and even when we called in the doctor, and he pronounced it bronchitis, I thought he would soon get over it; but at last it was forced upon me that he was dying.

I am thankful to-day that I had work during his illness, which took a lot off my mind. Each forenoon, after he was carefully bathed, he would call for his "fings," as he named his toys; but he soon let them slide out of his hands, and turned his languid gaze to his mother. I pass over the closing scenes; all was done that could be done; his mother was satisfied that day and night she had always been ready to his call, and I had this one solace, that I had some work, which enabled me to pay the doctor's bill and all the expenses of interment—no slight matter with the poor.

Looking back to those times, I see him in his characteristic attitude, standing at the open door, holding the door with one hand and watching the children at play, but ready to dart in to his mother if he saw anything strange; and I say it was all for the best.

CHAPTER XXIII

THE TIDE TURNS

ONCE again I had a proof of the saying, " After a storm comes a calm," for the next eighteen months found me fairly well employed, considering the general state of trade. I became acquainted with a Scotchman who belonged to Dumbarton. We were working together, when he mentioned the exponential theorem. I said: "You are the first man that I have heard mention that at work." We compared notes; he had been in France, Belgium, and part of Germany. He praised the working classes of Germany and Belgium, and in particular the harmony that existed amongst them. He stated that the Platt-Deutsch resembled (in sound) the lowland Scotch so much that he had little difficulty in understanding it.

On telling him that I was acquainted with the German language, he commenced to recite the ballad of the Erl König. I said: "Stop that, or we shall be put down for two lunatics!" But as we went home that evening we discussed several questions. His father, of whom he spoke with great admiration, had a great fancy for pure geometry, and he himself had (under his father)

202

studied Euclid pretty thoroughly. He expressed himself as delighted with meeting a fellow-workman who had similar tastes, and strongly urged me to take him as a lodger. I said I never had taken a lodger, and did not intend to. Lodgers were for widows and old people. But I would be very glad to see him any evening.

As the Yankees say, he froze to me, and his companionship made a great part of the summer glide past with rapidity. He was pleased with my eldest (and then only) boy's powers as a reader, and when I told him the boy had never been at school, he expressed his surprise.

Strange compound—he had all the Scotchman's perseverance, and ambition to succeed, but yet he would spend his earnings freely on drink. One evening he turned up unexpectedly. His father, who was a foreman mason at some ironworks, at Maryport, in Cumberland, I think, had broken his collar-bone. He must set off at once, and leave me to look after his tools and send them on. Strong man that he was, and inured to life's buffetings, he cried like a child on leaving me. I heard no more of him for a long time. At last a letter came from him. He was working at a church at Cromford, Derbyshire.

I replied to it at once, and expressed my pleasure at hearing from him, and hoped that he would write regularly, but I never heard from him again.

Employment continued fairly good for some time after the departure of the Scotchman, and I enjoyed a slight change from the everlasting anxieties attending being out of work. My eldest boy was now six years old, and I looked forward to training his young mind as a pleasant occupation, involving nothing more than directing his reading and drawing him out by discussion. Once or twice the School Board Officer had spoken to me about the boy not going to school. I told him that I intended him to go to school when he was a little older and stronger, and that in the meantime anyone who would trouble themselves to examine him would find that he was as far advanced as the average boy who attended regularly.

The official spoke very fairly, and said that his duty required him to make inquiries into the matter. He felt confident that the boy was being well educated, but, at the same time, advised me to send him as soon as possible, for his own sake, saying that the others would look upon him as a sort of outsider.

I thanked him, and before leaving this subject would just mention that my policy was successful, and that, thanks to the fresh air and exercise, I had no trouble with the boy's health.

It was now the year 1882, and our youngest boy was born, and by a strange coincidence I received a letter from Aunt Kate at Mosston, saying that her daughter had died. On comparing notes I found that my cousin had died at the same hour that my son was born. Brave Aunt Kate! her daughter had married a man in a good position, and everything pointed to a happy and prosperous life. My aunt had entertained the whole of Mosston on that day, and the village was in a state of unusual excitement.

One son was born from this marriage, and Aunt Kate's joy and pride in her grandson was unbounded. But a small cloud was already on the horizon. Her son - in - law's position was threatened by impending legislation, though the blow did not fall till a few years had elapsed. Even then he received a sum of money on being deprived of his position that might have set him up in some business. But his position, practically a sinecure, had unfitted him for the struggle necessary now to get a living, and my cousin, who had never been strong, broke down altogether, and died in the old house at Mosston.

My aunt had nursed her all through her gradual decline, and now was occupied with the future of her son-in-law and grandson. But we shall hear of them in due course.

For six weeks after the birth of our last child I had employment, and then I was again flung out. And now commenced a long and gradual series of untoward events, each one leaving me a little deeper in the mire. At first, having been pretty well employed for a good bit, we did not suffer much, and I kept looking forward to another job, but I was always too late or too soon. Week followed week, and month succeeded month, and still no job, although I had one or two days' work. I was obliged to fall back on my old shifts to get a little food.

I printed the name and address on some grocer's almanacs, for which he gave me a lot of bacon. I filled up a lot of emigration papers for people who were going out to Australia and New Zealand—in short, I tried all and every scheme that I could think of to obtain a little money. My wife did her utmost, and, in fact, almost more than is credible, to keep our heads above water all through the winter.

I now come to the turning-point of my life. I used to wake early in the morning, and yet dread to get up, as it meant burning the few coals we had. The two boys slept sound enough; and whilst I lay there I began to reckon myself up, and came to the conclusion that I was a dismal failure.

How were we existing? Only by the superhuman efforts of my wife, whose broken utterances in her sleep showed that her mind was filled with the one thought—to get a little work finished that would bring in a few pence.

I determined that I would (this word should be written WOULD) make a change. We had struggled through the depth of the winter, and the spring was approaching. I never breathed a syllable of my determination, but it was there, nor did I deceive myself by any day-dreams. The Yankees have a saying that "there is no great loss without some small gain"; and poverty had taught us how to make the most of a shilling.

There are always some paltry jobs to be picked up by the casual worker that are unnoticed by the man who has a regular job. But these jobs are done at the lowest possible price by someone who is gasping for a few shillings. Although I despised myself as a failure, I felt that if I had one chance more I would make the most of it. I was in that frame of mind described by the common phrase " You just want a start."

The thing was to get that first start. I made a start, and as it turned out to be, though small in itself, the turn of the tide, I will briefly describe it.

Where we lived at that time was in the vicinity of two quarries, one of which has since been filled in and built upon. One of these quarries produced a stone very much superior to the other. This latter was being worked by two men whom I knew, and was the quarry where the man fell down at his work and died, as I have already stated

A local contractor had to supply some stones for the corporation. I asked him for a job to dress them. He said that he could get them ready dressed for two shillings each from the quarry which produced the best stone. This at the time was a staggerer, though now I rather doubt its truth. But I went to the quarry I knew, and made arrangements with the quarrymen, so that the price of the material and my labour came to one shilling and eightpence; and besides, this was the nearest quarry, and the cost of transport was less.

I secured the job, and I am thankful to say that from that time, although I have often been out of work, I have never once known the pinch of poverty.

This was in the spring of 1883. Four years after this, in the Queen's Jubilee year, I was coming home from work with an old pal who had been seeking a job, but did not get one. He was a bachelor, and rather independent in his ways.

We talked of work and seeking work, and incidentally the name of this contractor cropped up. My pal said that once, about four years ago, he had asked this contractor for a job, and he (the contractor) said: "Go away. I am getting it done for less than nothing." Stopping short, I said: "I am the fellow that was doing it for less than nothing, and yet I could earn tenpence per hour at it. That is more than wages." As the man I was speaking to knew me well, and also the local prices, I explained how it was done, and he saw it clearly. But everything did not run smoothly even on this first job.

When I went to the contractor's house for my first wages, his wife grumbled at me for coming to the front-door. But her words made not the slightest impression. I had made a start, and my resolution was beginning to take effect. I said nothing to anyone, but after a little time I had a never-failing source of secret amusement in noting the gradual change of tone amongst my neighbours.

I paid off all my little debts, and secured a job that lasted for five months. I now had the pleasure of purchasing some clothes for my wife, that were a very slight reward for her heroic fight with adversity. I shall never forget the pleasure I had one Saturday night, as my wife and I called in at a large draper's shop. The shop was crowded, and a lot of the customers knew my wife well.

I stood at the door, for I hate shopping, but I could hear the conversation inside. One or two neighbours were saying, "Isn't Mrs. —— looking well? What a change!" One part of my secret resolve was never to breathe a word that I had turned over a fresh leaf, as that would spoil the pleasure I was having.

Towards the end of this five months' job I had a surprise. I met a man whose face seemed familiar. I stopped, and he did the same. It was my cousin at Mosston, Aunt Kate's only son. But what a change! He was prematurely old, and evidently nearing his end, which came about twelve months after. I never hinted that he was looking ill. He told me that he had come into the town to try hot baths; and I called to see him on the Saturday afternoon, and took my eldest son for him to see. It was the last time that I saw him alive.

On leaving the house I met a man whom I knew, a builder's foreman. He said: "Are you working?" And I replied: "Yes, but I could do with a better job." He said his firm had a lot of

14

work to let, and that if my price was suitable he would recommend me for character. In short, I got the job, which turned out a good one, and I should never have heard of it if I hadn't gone to see my cousin. The new job was at a village outside of the city; but, as workmen's trains had come into vogue, I had no trouble in reaching it; and, after having worked there a few months, I took a house, and left the district in which we had lived ever since our marriage. As the town was extending towards this village, I had very little farther to travel on an average, and I had the benefit of the fresh air for the boys. We lived for fourteen years and a half in this new district, so that my choice was pretty well tested.

We were now living in the country, and the change of scene, together with pure country milk, worked wonders with our two children. We had been in our new home about three months, and I was working in the town, or rather just on the outskirts, when a letter came with the news of the death of my cousin at Mosston. As it was an awkward place to reach, owing to its distance from any railway, my wife brought me the letter on to the job, and I had just time to catch the last train in that direction.

It was only by running by a near cut and flinging myself over a stone wall that I caught the train. After a run on the main line, I reached the junction, where the train was waiting to proceed in the direction of Mosston. Seventeen years had passed since I had visited the place, and even the branch line on which I was travelling had been opened since.

After a few miles were traversed the old familiar outlines of the changeless hills began to show themselves. I was glad there were very few passengers in the train, for I was not in any humour for conversation. It was August in 1884, and the weather was glorious. On arriving at the terminus, I set out on the well-known old road, and reached Mosston about ten o'clock at night.

As the public-house closed at ten, there were only a few near relatives of the deceased in the house. Aunt Kate seemed not one day older— the same firm step, the same substantial figure, the same bluish-grey eyes—only the voice was (owing to the sad occasion) somewhat less firm than of old. The interment was on the next day. After a few inquiries amongst the different relatives, I went to rest, and in the morning took a look round the village.

Several houses had disappeared, and the population was not half what it used to be. Only one of the Davisons, the carriers, was alive ; the only familiar figure that met my eyes was the old blacksmith. I went into the smithy, and had a talk with his son, who had never married. The daughter had married, and the old blacksmith set himself down to rock the cradle of his grandchild with a piece of string, long enough to permit him to sit in the smithy and hear the news. He smiled at me and said : " This is all I am good for now."

The smithy window looked into the garden, un-changed save that there were now no beehives. The blacksmith's vice was just in front of the window. When a boy I had turned the handle of this vice till it had dropped seemingly in two pieces, and I had run for bare life.

We had a laugh over the memory of my childish fears, and dread of horses, and I left the smithy, and proceeded to call on an old friend, a shoemaker. The shoemaker's shop was full, for, besides customers, there were people who had simply called to gossip about the funeral, which was sure to bring together a number of people who had formerly lived in the district. I found the old shoemaker hale and hearty, and eager as ever to talk of anything, from burials to the affairs of the nation

CHAPTER XXIV

WITH THE FLOWING TIDE

BY this time the various relatives were beginning to arrive. The churchyard was a few miles off, still farther up among the hills, and nobody was going on foot. Aunt Kate did not go herself to the churchyard, and I shall not attempt to describe the scene as her only son was taken out of the house. Her grandson was, of course, her representative, and her son-in-law was also with him in the leading vehicle. It was a glorious August day, and, for the most of the journey, the pace was very slow, as we were ascending the hills.

The church was a small one, on a hillside near to a plantation. Just before the body was committed to the earth, there was a short shower, and when the sun shone out bright after the rain, a cloud of small flies came out of the plantation, and attacked the bare-headed mourners with such vigour that the clergyman had to hold his book in his left hand and flourish a pocket-handkerchief continually with his right.

The horses standing harnessed in the vehicles were almost driven frantic, and some of them which were in the traces lay down and rolled in

the road.   As soon as possible we all seated ourselves again, and when we had left the churchyard out of sight the pace became swifter and
swifter.   I was seated in a brake that was hired
from the nearest town, and the driver said that, if
racing was going to be the game, he would not be
last, and towards the end of the journey we flew
down some of the banks, and I expected that there
would be a spill.   But the driver managed to land
us all right, though the rear of one vehicle was
rammed with the pole of another.

After a dinner, the most of the relatives set off
at once, but I came home the next day.   Aunt
Kate made me promise to come, with my wife and
the two boys, to see her.   We came about two
months afterwards; the weather was still abnor-
mally fine.   We had to hire a vehicle of some
sort (there are so many different names) for the
last stage of the journey, and Aunt Kate actually
expressed her surprise that I should have incurred
this expense.

Good old soul! she never thought that my wife
was not used to carrying a child about ten or
fifteen miles across the hills.   But she made my
wife and the boys heartily welcome, and, by a
strange coincidence, my eldest was now eight
years old, exactly my age when I first came to
Mosston in the carrier's cart.   But the Davison
that had brought me was dead, and his brother
was getting feeble.

I came home on the Monday following the
Saturday night on which we had arrived.   As I

set away from my aunt's door, I saw my eldest boy standing, fishing in the brook, and I thought of the changes that had taken place since I had played, at his age, by the same brook.

My wife and the two boys came to the terminus a day or so later, in the baker's cart, in the real old country style. To this day they speak of Aunt Kate's send-off—stuffing the boys' hands with something to eat. Her son-in-law stayed at Mosston, and partly filled the blank caused by my cousin's death.

Two years flew past. I was well employed, and the two boys were in good health, and I now placed the eldest at school. He was put in the fourth standard, and soon was at home with the other boys, and his mother had the pleasure of seeing him on Sundays with a surplice, singing in the choir. I was now passing through the happiest days. I had plenty of work, and enjoyed my books in the evening. My wife was proud of my boy's success in the school, and looking forward to placing our youngest there, as soon as he was five years old. As I understood music, I bought a harmonium, and set my youngest boy to it. For instruction book I used Czerny's "School of Velocity," which I had bought as waste-paper for twopence.

In a twelvemonth he could rattle off these exercises as fast as the instrument could speak, though he was slightly bothered with some of the runs extending beyond the compass of the instrument. But I had to cut my coat according to my cloth, and a harmonium was, of course, much cheaper than a piano. My wife's father was very fond of music, and played himself on the violin. He used to sit, and never take his eyes off my boy's hands, as he ran up and down the keyboard. Then I got a couple of books of overtures, arranged for the piano and violin, and, by dint of practising together, we were enabled to play some of them at the concerts given in the school-room.

Thus, working regularly through the day, and employing the evenings in teaching a few extra subjects to my eldest boy, the months slipped away rapidly and pleasantly.

The year 1887, the year of the Queen's Jubilee, found me working in a new atmosphere altogether, for I got a job to work as a mason at the local gaol. In various ways the job was a very unpleasant one, as it consisted in cutting passages in the old stone walls, covered with accumulated coats of whitewash, the dust of which was very annoying, and in gradually remodelling the internal structure, in accordance with modern ideas.

Thus there was very little sunlight or fresh air; but I soon became interested in the new world to be found inside the gaol gates. The gaol was not one of those to which long-time prisoners are sent, and I soon came to the conclusion that to the majority of the inmates the greatest punishment would be to set them outside and keep them there. This may seem strange, but I am more than ever convinced of the truth of it. There is no doubt but that any of them are glad to get out for a short time. The various organizations for helping discharged prisoners will partly account for that, and besides, there are always some ready to stand a few drinks to a discharged prisoner, who can give in return some news of a pal, or a son, or a brother inside; but, sooner or later, the fact is borne home to the late prisoner that he cannot get a living outside, that, in fact, he is deficient in those qualities which bring success, and he gravitates, naturally, to the prison again.

Human nature is such that there are many who would rather let it be thought they are confirmed criminals, and that they cannot resist the temptation to steal, than own that they cannot earn their living in the fierce competition outside.

Let anyone scan the daily papers closely, and he will soon see that some of the clumsy thefts therein described, and the utter fatuity of some of the attempted crimes, can only be understood on the theory that the criminals wanted to be locked up. The first morning that I started I was full of curiosity, as I stood outside the gaol gates at half-past six in the morning.

The gates were opened, and locked behind me. I found myself under the vaulted roof of a gateway, large enough to admit a horse and cart. A gate, formed of strong iron bars, was between me and the inner courtyard of the prison. Another tower at the top of a flight of steps was directly in front, and two curtain walls connected this

tower with the gateway under which I was
standing. The porter unlocked the inner gate,
and we went into the courtyard, and through
ordinary doors to the right and left in these
curtain walls we passed to our various occupations.

Some of the prisoners were labouring to us,
but they took it very easily, and paid more attention to the orders of the warder who was over
them than they did to our foreman. If the
slightest shower came on, the warder said, " Fall
in," and they marched Indian file into their cells.

On being shown a large stone upon which I
was to start, I took off my coat and set to work;
but before many minutes had elapsed, a warder
came round, and started to lecture me on the
enormity of leaving my coat there. Perhaps a
letter was in one of the pockets, and any of the
prisoners could take it out. I must either keep it
on, or let it be locked up in a room where we got
our breakfasts. But if a shower came on, I would
be wet through before I could get a warder to go
with me to get it; so I decided to work with it on,
like the prisoners.

I found some of the prisoners jolly fellows to
work with, but there were some who were
different. If any female prisoners came past
(always accompanied by a female warder) all the
male prisoners had to stand with their faces to
the wall till they had passed into the next courtyard. In one respect all the prisoners were alike:
they were always begging, either for food, or
tobacco, or something.

One day one of the prisoners asked me for a match. I told him I didn't smoke. He said: "Bring me some to-morrow." Not wishing to deny him point-blank, I said that the matches we used were safety ones, and that he would not be able to strike them. "Oh yes, I can; I can strike them on my slate in the cell. I was smoking all day on Sunday up the ventilator."

Giving the prisoners tobacco was an offence strictly punishable, and they got none from me, although I plead guilty to having sometimes left some food in the gas-meter, for whoever chose to find it. One thing was very noticeable, and that was the care taken of the prisoners' health.

One morning, on one of them asking me, as usual, how things were going, I happened to say that I felt a little out of sorts, as my youngest boy had a slight fever, and I had been kept awake a good part of the night. He at once looked round and said: "Don't let the warder hear you, or you will be sent off home at once." "Why?" "Why, for fear any of us catch it." "But it is nothing." "Never mind, there will be a whole lot of bother about it." One of the prisoners was a very obliging, lively young fellow, and different from all the rest in really taking a pleasure in work. He was allowed a little more latitude than the ordinary.

Part of the labour consisted of breaking stones, and to look at the prisoners whilst they were thus engaged, no one would have thought it hard labour. The entrance of any fresh prisoners always caused a slight ripple of excitement, and one day I was astonished to see the gate open, and a Salvation Army official come in, with the red waistcoat and gold crown. Even the governor relaxed a little from his dignity, and came to see how this came about.

As usual, the explanation was very simple. There had been a Salvation Army procession somewhere, and this official had been walking alongside with one glove off. A boy was making himself objectionable, and was given a slight tap with the glove by him. The boy's father had taken him to court, and a rather severe fine had been imposed by the Bench. As the alternative was only seven days, the official, either through motives of economy, or else by way of practical protest against the decision of the Bench, elected to do the seven days.

I was just beginning to get accustomed to the little restrictions and the routine of the place, when one forenoon, about ten o'clock, there was a commotion. Some of the workmen had either given some tobacco to the prisoners, or else the latter had got it from the men's coats. This could be done. Anyhow, we were all severely talked to, and warned for the future. The governor, though very strict, was kind-hearted, or we would, perhaps, have been instantly "sacked." Those prisoners whose time had expired were let out in the morning about eight o'clock, and a representative of the Discharged Prisoners' Aid Society gave some of them a little money, and paid railway fares for some of them. My work kept me near the gate, as the large stones were just brought through the gate into the courtyard, and after they were considerably lightened by being dressed to shape, they were transferred to their resting-place.

In this manner I was a daily witness of the ingress and egress of the prisoners, and soon noticed that, in the majority of cases, they seemed more jolly coming in than going out. This may have been partly due to bravado, but none the less this was the fact, and first put me on the track of the idea that the majority of them looked upon the prison as their home, and the hardest punishment would be to keep them outside. Inside they had cleanliness, regular food, exercise, and isolation, ensuring them sufficient air-space, and as the most of them suffered from those chronic diseases brought on by dirt and neglect, diseases which are most amenable to regularity of treatment, they looked upon the place as a hospital.

One amusing feature of the life within those high walls was to see the food brought to those on remand. A pint of beer (which must be in a glass bottle) was, I think, the limit in the liquor direction, but I have seen a pie, big enough for six, brought by some poor woman for some man who could not possibly eat it all. The poor woman would most likely think that what he did not eat would go to some other prisoner, and it would have been cruel to undeceive her.

Some of the warders, when they got to know me, offered to show me (during the dinner hour) the place of execution, and a few of the fixtures connected therewith, but I thanked them, and said I had not the slightest curiosity about them.

All things come to an end, and so did the job on which I was working. My employer finished the work he had contracted for, and some other contractor took another part of the prison to alter. Once more I found myself outside, but the conclusions formed from what I saw inside remain unshaken to this day.

CHAPTER XXV

AMONGST THE MINERS

By one of life's contrasts my next job was right out in the glorious sunlight. It was now the year of the Queen's Jubilee, a regular hot summer. There was a colliery a few miles from where I lived, and the most of the miners had shares in a local Co-operative Society. As the colliery was surrounded by a compact working-class population, they had come to the conclusion to build an establishment for their own use, instead of travelling two or three miles to the central establishment.

These miners were a study; their language would betray them anywhere as miners, and on the days when for some reason or other they did not go down the mine, they came and sat, crouched on their heels, all over the building. As they were really, though indirectly, our employers, they were tolerated, although sometimes they were sadly in the way.

I must say that I have never heard politics discussed with more force and directness than among these men, and they certainly knew what they wanted, which is more than some people do.

Their debates, couched in the very plainest English, were interesting to follow, and differed totally from the vague generalities and hackneyed phrases heard when an M.P. addresses a meeting of working men. All this struck me because, in our own trade, politics, as a rule, were left to so-called "cranks," the only measure really noticed being the Employers' Liability Bill.

The workmen's houses were in rows on the side of a hill opening to the south, and the houses all had extensive gardens in front. The new building was on the roadside, and soon became the Trafalgar Square where everything was discussed.

As the summer became hotter and hotter, I took lodgings for a few weeks during the hottest time, though I could, and did, walk the distance before and after. I thus became a spectator of the indoor life of a class of men who certainly are distinguished by the force and vigour which they put into anything they turn their attention to. A brass band was one of the features of the place, and the men often sat on the grass and practised in the evenings. This, however, was one of the subjects on which I held views which were regarded as worse than heresy by the average brass bandsman.

An accident happened shortly after I took lodgings at this colliery. One morning, as the cage was descending, one of the men got fast between the cage and the guides on which it slides. Fortunately, he was not killed, and was almost fit for work again in a few weeks, which says a good deal for the soundness of his constitution. But all the miners seemed hard as nails, and fit for any amount of hardship. They were paid once a fortnight on the Fridays, and the whole place was like a fair on the pay Friday evenings, as tradesmen of all descriptions came out from the town and seemed to do a satisfactory trade. The next Saturday was always called "pay Saturday," and on that day the miners did not work.

Taking all things into consideration, those miners, with their short hours and good pay, their houses, with only an acknowledgment for rent, and their allowances of coal, seemed to me to have reached the high-water mark of industrial prosperity; and the most striking thing about them was the fact that they had gained their advantages by organization.

With the approach of winter the job was finished (at least, for the masons), and I returned to my old haunts. I pass over three or four years, which seemed to glide past, with nothing to cause a ripple on the smooth stream of prosperity. I was well employed, and devoted my spare hours to perfecting my knowledge of French and German.

One slight or strange event, according as the reader chooses to view it, I will mention here, as it occurred during these three or four years. I dare say there are few people who have not had one or two strange experiences bordering upon the supernatural in their lifetime. I have had one or two, and one of them a tragical one, which seemed to bear upon the Scotch idea of being "fey." This one, though connected with a death, had nothing tragic about it, and was unattended with any vague testimony.

My wife had been attending a woman who was connected by marriage, and who was on her death-bed. As this woman was no relation of mine, I was not at all anxious about her illness, although I placed no hindrance in the way when my wife went to see her. I mention this to show that my mind was not on the subject at all.

It was about the latter end of March, and at that time it was daylight when I got up to go to work. My two boys slept in a bed in the kitchen, and my wife and I slept in a cheap iron bed in another room.

I was aroused one morning by a curious feeling, as if I had been awakened up by a loud noise, and yet I had not the slightest idea what the noise was like. While I was collecting my senses I heard another noise, and, though I could see nothing at all unusual, I could describe this noise exactly. It was just as if someone had struck the iron bedstead with a heavy piece of wood, so as to make it ring.

With that my wife woke, and said: "What is that, making that noise?" It was just daylight, and I said, quite calmly (to avoid her being frightened): "I don't know, but I am just going to see about it." I passed through into the kitchen, and my eldest boy, who was always sound asleep when I got up, was sitting up in his bed. He said : " Who's that going about banging all the doors ?"

I went into the yard, but could neither see nor hear anything. When I entered the kitchen, my boy was already asleep again, and, as it was about time to get up for work, I told my wife that I could neither see nor hear anything, and that I was going to work.

I went, and when my son brought my dinner, he brought the news that the woman was dead, and I found, on getting home, that she had died exactly at the time we were all awakened by the noises.

The other experience took place many years before the time of which I write, but I put it down here as a sort of parallel to the last incident.

I am aware that it is exceedingly difficult to express in words the peculiar feeling which seizes us when some calamity is hanging over anyone in our company. It may be that the individual is literally in the shadow of death, and that his actions, seen through this shadow, strike us as being strange and unearthly.

We have all, at some time or other, seen some well-known object through a fog, or some peculiar atmospheric condition which made it almost unrecognizable.

" He must be going to die " is an expression heard every day, when someone has done something quite foreign to his usual conduct.

The Scotch have a short expression for this conduct. It is, " He must be 'fey.'"

At one time I boarded with a family who lived about a quarter of a mile outside of a village. The house and grounds were their own property. The head of the family was in business in the village, and only came in to meals through the day.

The family (a fairly large one) was composed of grown-up sons and daughters, and one little boy, and a girl, a few years his senior. A brook flowed through the grounds, close past the back of the house, and a railway bridge was in course of construction over this brook. I was employed on this bridge, and had boarded with the family for some time, and was quite at home. Whatever was the reason I cannot say, but this youngest boy, who was a pet, and slightly spoilt, never spoke to me, or would let me touch him, if he could help it. At first I wondered, but, after a time, I took no notice of his conduct, and almost forgot his existence. I have mentioned " The Wide, Wide World " in these pages, and that it was the first book of which I remember the title. As a boy I read this book, and I noticed the passage where Van Brunt fell and injured himself, and little Ellen had to saddle her pony and go for assistance. I had commented on this passage, and said how unlikely it was that there was no one available but little Ellen. But experience teaches, and on the day of which I am now speaking both father and mother and all the grown-up members of the family were absent through various causes, although the absence of some of them was only temporary.

Only the little girl and boy and myself were on the place. The works were stopped for the winter, and the brook was slightly swollen with the melted snow.

As usual, I was buried in a book, and the house was perfectly still, for the little boy and girl were playing in the pale spring sunshine outside.

I went outside for a minute, to look after one or two little things that I knew required to be done, in the absence of the family. Having seen that everything was in order, I was returning into the house, and had almost reached the door, when a ball came towards me, thrown either by the boy or girl.

I caught the ball, and flung it to the girl, who flung it to the little boy, who, in his turn, again flung it to me.

This took place two or three times, when the thought came into my mind: How strange for the boy to be playing with me.

This thought caused me to look at the boy, for, in playing with the ball, my eyes had been following its course. I was struck at once with his expression, and asked him if he was crying. "No."

Was he ill? "No."

Seeing that he did not like being questioned, and knowing his peculiar nature, I said no more, but entered the house, and resumed my book.

It seemed to me only two or three minutes, when I heard a scream. I flung down the book, and ran out.

At the door I met the girl, who said: "—— is in the brook!" and, without stopping to give one word as to where he fell in, or anything, darted for the village, and I was left absolutely alone on the place, with the knowledge that the little boy was in the brook.

The brook was swollen and very deep in some places, but if the little girl had had the presence of mind to keep her eye on the boy, and rely on her scream bringing me out, he might have been saved. As it happened, he was past help when found, for the body had been swept under some bushes.

I never wish to have another time like that which I spent before some of the family arrived from the village. Of course, I said nothing about being struck with the boy's expression, and, if the incident had been unique, I would not mention it here. But it was only the most distinct among others, which, if related, would make these passages appear a string of anecdotes.

Though we lived in the country, and were surrounded by a purely industrial population, yet the same forces were at work, producing the same tragedies, as are generally associated with the slums of the greatest cities. A workman who lived two or three doors from us left his house one morning to go to his work. He was seen and spoken to by a woman, and yet he was found not a hundred yards off, a few minutes later, dead.

What is more, the police could never get the slightest clue to the mystery. As it was daylight at the time, and I was known to go out regularly, I was asked by the police whether I had seen any suspicious person about, but I had seen no one.

The town, on whose outskirts we lived, kept growing at an abnormal rate in our direction, and I was regularly employed by one builder in the new streets. As I was improving in my prospects, I went about a bit more than usual, and I chanced to come across the young man of whom I spoke in a former chapter, who had come for lessons at sixpence per week, but did not turn up on Friday night, when the money was due. I said that he would turn up again, and that the laugh would be against him.

Well, we entered into conversation; he was full of confidence and boast of his position and prospects. He was a young man, and had a room (taken from his mother) where he kept all his books and drawing instruments. He was expecting a job as a colliery under-manager soon. I listened to it all, but I knew that he could not read the mathematical formulæ found in the books used by colliery managers. At last he got at me. "Why didn't I get myself into some better position? If I hadn't ambition to apply for a foreman or manager's job, why didn't I write to papers and get paid, like he did?"

At this I pricked up my ears. I was used to

being asked: "Why didn't I do this or that?"—everybody is asked that, and takes it for what it is worth; but this man writing to trade papers, and being paid for it. I would for once sift this to the bottom. I asked him to what paper he had written. "The *English Mechanic*, and they paid well—at the rate of eightpence per inch." This sounded like business, but I had my doubts. I arranged to call and see him on the next Sunday.

I went, and after a little talk we went upstairs to his own room, and I asked to see his articles in the *English Mechanic.*

After a good deal of pressing he hunted up some correspondence, and gave me a letter to read. It was from the *English Mechanic*, and after saying their columns were always open for contributions by practical workmen, it proceeded to deal with something he had sent, and was advising him not to repeat the same thing so many times.

So this was all. I felt angry with myself for being so persistent, but I had had so many indirect sneers and hints that So-and-so was doing this, and why couldn't I? that it was no wonder I got out of patience. I turned the conversation, for I saw he felt humiliated, although it was the result of his own boasting.

CHAPTER XXVI

YEARS OF PLENTY

FROM the time of Joseph there have always been fat and lean years. I had gone through some lean ones, and now was passing through some fat ones. I have said little about the trivial details of daily labour, but the trade was now so different from what it had been that it calls for some remarks.

In all large towns there are always what are called outside jobs in the building trade, such as new houses by speculating builders in the suburbs. The town with which I had been connected so long was now become a city, and was growing faster than ever. Often in the past a halfpenny per hour extra had been paid to banker hands on these new buildings, because the sheds were not so good, and there was more lifting, and generally the men were expected to do more work—and they did.

But now a penny per hour extra was quite common, and on some jobs more was paid, though I never got more than the extra penny. A number of banker hands had gone to South Africa—the Cape, as they called it; and fabulous reports of making thirty shillings a day were coming from them. Rents were rising rapidly, and a great change had come over the style of ordinary work-men's dwellings. Formerly bay-windows in cut stone were only seen in what are called self-contained houses—that is, those which have upstairs and down occupied by the same tenant; but now streets of workmen's houses in flats, with double bay-windows upstairs and down, in cut stone, were being built, and what is more, were being immediately let at six shillings and sixpence and seven shillings per week per flat.

The local quarries could not supply the stone fast enough, and stone was brought from any-where within fifty miles to supply the demand. The huge engineering shops and factories were increasing their employés by thousands, and workmen were coming (mostly from the southern counties) to fill up the new workshops and occupy the new houses.

I had been for a long time in the employ of a small builder, who had gone so far as to say that I had set him on his feet. If so, he did not show much gratitude, for now, when he was prospering, he began to put on airs; and although any of the bricklayers or labourers could get what is called " sub "—that is, money in advance—yet if I asked for any, he said: "You don't drink; you need no money."

For a long time past I had been offered employ-ment by various builders, but I had stuck to the same man, partly because I did not wish to throw up constant work, and partly because in the past he had been a good employer; but now he was spoilt by prosperity. What was unusual was that he was a banker hand himself, for ninety per cent. of the builders are joiners; but he did not care about the banker.

He said that the stone dust affected his lungs; but some of his men were irreverent enough to say that all that he knocked off would not affect anyone. He was almost a total abstainer, but the boozers on his job (and he had some) could always get money and beer for the asking.

One good point about him was that he kept his men well. Two bricklayers had been with him from the time that he started to build for himself, and I had worked for him long before that, when he was only a sub-contractor.

The men used to laugh at his simplicity, but I told them he would laugh at them at the finish, and he did so. He had some original methods: he would come out first thing in the mornings, and if (as often happened) the labourers were not out, he would take the hod and carry bricks and lime to the bricklayers. If, on the other hand, a bricklayer was late, he would take a trowel and lay bricks to keep the labourer fully employed.

Then, when all hands were fairly set away, he would take it easy.

Sometimes he would help me at the banker, always taking care that the wind blew the dust away from him, though, if we were dressing a long stone, this meant that I had all the dust to deal with. Still, as I had been so long with him, I had a few privileges.

Thus the time went on, each year showing a more marked difference in the style of the workmen's houses. Let me say here that a house always means a flat unless special mention is made of self-contained houses. A few years before about the only stonework in these flats was stone heads and sills to the windows and doors, and stone string course underneath cornice, and the stone cornice; but now the doors were surrounded with stone, technically called door-casing, and besides the cut-stone bay-windows the houses had little gardens in front with cut-stone coping to the dwarf brick walls enclosing them. The sanitary arrangements were become infinitely superior, two or three tenants no longer using the same washhouse or lavatory. Of course, all this meant the rents of these flats going from three shillings and sixpence per week up to seven shillings and sixpence. But another thing that was making a great change amongst the workmen was the working of the Employers' Liability Bill.

Formerly it was quite customary to see labourers staggering up a ladder, carrying a window-head or a sill balanced on their shoulders, using both hands to grasp the sides (not the rungs) of the ladders. Stepping off the ladder on to the scaffold with the stone on their shoulders was the crucial difficulty. After the passing of the Bill, the next step was raising these stones (with one side resting on the ladder) by four men, two at each end having hold of ropes passed round the stones.

Once my employer was having some cornice drawn up like this, each piece weighing about 350 pounds. Two bricklayers stood on the scaffold at one side of the ladder, and a labourer and myself at the other side. The stones were brought forward and leant against the ladder, the ropes passed round them, and we all commenced to pull our best.

Now, unfortunately the contempt which the workmen have for theory or science endangers their lives continually.

I have never once seen workmen employed in this manner all pulling steadily, so as to keep the stone level, and the weight evenly distributed on both sides, but instead of that they started with a jerk and continued, each side striving to get their end up first (thus throwing most of the weight on to the other side). Meanwhile such compliments as "Get some beef into you!" "Is there anybody pulling at that side?" etc., would be freely bandied about.

In our case I admit that our end was soon the lowest, but resolution or will-power is no use against weight, in the purely mechanical problem of lifting. But in my comrade's and my own frantic struggles to keep our end up, the rope (a rotten one) broke, and I fell backwards across the scaffold and landed across the brick wall, ready to receive the cornice.

Had I been standing before an opening for a window, it would have been death or crippled for life. I made this my last attempt at this sort of thing, and soon after the practice became almost universal of using pulley - blocks. The latest fashion, in this district at least, is to use a peculiar pulley working with a long rope half an inch in section. It is said to be a Yankee invention. When the stone is ready for lowering, a string is pulled and the stone comes down very quickly.

No one can foresee the consequences of a new Act of Parliament, and the Liability Act has, in the building trade, made a marked change amongst the labourers. Strength is no longer the principal qualification, and a boozer, who would at one time count upon his numerous shortcomings being condoned for the sake of his prowess when the heavy lifting came on, now finds that he must keep time or else leave.

I had now come to that time of life when one begins to look round himself, and see how he stands in the great race for existence. I saw most of my contemporary workmen beginning to fail, and those of my old pals who were still knocking about seeking for easy berths.

Nothing has ever struck me more than the fact (never mentioned in books to my knowledge) that a workman if he knows or thinks he knows anything more than usual at once strives to leave his trade. As the saying is, "You must keep your coat on, or you will never make your fortune." This does not say much for the dignity of labour. There are one or two things that can only be learnt by experience extending over a long space of time, and I state emphatically that

England is becoming rapidly a sober nation, and that every day strength counts for less and brains for more in the battle of life.

About this time the footwalks in front of the houses were flagged, now they are mostly cemented. A local contractor who still follows street-making used to employ some men constantly squaring and laying these flags. Amongst them I had often remarked a young fellow not out of his time. I had never spoken to him or, indeed, heard his voice, but his manner was quite different from all the rest.

As the street-flagging soon covered a good deal of ground, and therefore a shed was out of the question, he sometimes came into the houses on which I was employed, to shelter from the rain. One day I was cutting some holes inside for the joiners, when a smart shower drove him inside. He stood beside me for a few minutes, and when I had finished said: "Are you going to hear X—— to-night?" This was a great politician. I replied: "I would not go round the corner to hear him." He said: "I have to go, or I would not go myself." "How's that?" "I have some prizes to take, and must be there." I smiled at the neat way in which he had let us all know that he had some prizes to take. I knew X—— was going to present the prizes, but I had thought it was politics the young man wanted to talk about. The ice once broken, I found this young fellow was really a very hard student, and though his age put him out of the question as companion for myself, my eldest son was just coming into the trade as a joiner, and I thought this lad would be good company for him.

I told him I had done a little in his own line of study, and invited him for an evening. He came, and we kept up the acquaintance for some time, till he won a scholarship that took him right away from the district. The scholarship was a purely technical one; but as soon as the three years for which it was tenable had expired, he entered some training institution for the Methodist ministry. This was another instance of "You must keep your coat on, or you will never be anything." I think a skilled mechanic as good as a Methodist preacher, but everyone to his taste. In this case I am sure he was more cut out for a mechanic, for though really a hard student, he was not brilliant. My eldest boy had now determined on being a joiner, and started on the same job as myself under my old employer, but he only stayed a fortnight. The Friday before the Saturday on which he left my employer and I were working together at the banker. During the afternoon I said to him: "Where do you buy your hardware?" "What do you want to know that for?" "Because I must buy my son some joiner's tools, and thought that you could get them cheaper from your hardware merchant, and that I could repay you." I was amazed when he said quite coolly: "I don't think it is worth while; I never see him doing anything."

Recovering myself, I said : " All right; you and I have known each other long enough to understand one another. This is Friday afternoon ; he will be done to-morrow at twelve o'clock, and we'll say no more about it." I got him another place, but he did not stay long with this new employer, and at last I put him to the third, with whom he stayed and gave every satisfaction till this last employer gave up the business.

CHAPTER XXVII

MOSSTON REVISITED

THE safety bicycles had now become fairly common, and were making great changes in working men's lives. For in the building trade, where the jobs are scattered about, and not fixtures like factories, they were very handy for seeking jobs; and though at first they were very expensive, second-hand ones soon became pretty cheap, and travelling three or four miles night and morning was a pleasure.

I bought one, and after a short time I made up my mind to have a run to Mosston on it. The distance to Mosston was only about fifty miles, and to go by train almost occupied a whole day, as it lay off the main lines and the final stage had to be walked. I chose a Saturday afternoon during the longest days, as the rough roads made riding by lamplight bad on account of the surface stones.

I never wrote to say I was coming, and Aunt Kate was astonished when I came. I found Mosston changing rapidly now. The people had sadly diminished, the neighbouring farms had all been either bought by one large landholder or else leased by one farmer, who had laid almost all the land down to grass, and in some cases even the farmhouses themselves were falling to pieces, being unoccupied.

The natives had heard of the brisk times that had been experienced in the town, which was their word for the large city to which everybody seemed to gravitate sooner or later. I satisfied their curiosity, and was able to give them all the news.

A new generation had sprung up, the County Councils had been in existence for some time, and I was actually a witness of the phenomenon of hearing in the old kitchen farm-hands relating how they had put the screw on to one of the local landholders to make him put up proper sanitary conveniences for the cottages. After this I was not surprised when the conversation took a socialistic tone, but here I could not join in. I told them all that I had not studied the question, but that the little I had heard about it led me to think that it did not come under the head of practical politics.

I was surprised to see such a gathering of working men, all seeming to have plenty of money to spend on the Saturday night, especially as I had passed so many houses whose roofs had fallen in, being unoccupied. As usual on making inquiries, the explanation was very simple. Some of the local mansions were being enlarged and altered, and owing to the depopulation of the country, all the mechanics had to be brought from the town, and were paid about thirty per cent. more than would have been paid to the old school of estate masons and carpenters. Besides, being only, as they termed it, "birds of passage," they were in lodgings, and mostly single men.

I soon saw where the socialistic ideas had come from. Some of the natives told me that two or three farmers had driven in traps on the Sunday afternoon to the nearest large villages (I will not call them towns), and offered ten shillings a day for extra hands for a few days for the hay harvest. When the public-house closed, some of the men procured flasks of spirit, and turned out into the roads to go to their lodgings. As a brother "chip," I was invited to go with them, and very pleasant it was in the midsummer night. I could have almost floated in whisky if I had been inclined; but as it was in bottles, and all the men were more or less "elevated," they did not notice that, though I put the bottle to my lips, I merely swallowed a few drops.

One or two of the older ones knew me, and introduced me formally as being almost a native, and especially as being a nephew of the old landlady. That was enough; my hand was almost wrung off, and I only got away by promising the whole lot that I would visit them early on the Sunday morning.

We had reached a small footbridge over a stream about half a mile from my aunt's house, and some sat on the handrail, while others flung themselves down on the grass; but these were speedily roused by the elder ones, who knew that meant falling asleep, and perhaps a chill.

At last the final good-nights were said, and I was left alone. I reached the top of a small rise, at the foot of which this stream flowed, and I could see the few chimneys and steep, tiled roofs of Mosston. I stood and leant on a gate by the roadside. The murmur of the stream reached my ears. Close to the bridge was a pool, into which, as a boy, I had jumped, on seeing some cows come towards me, and was laughed at for a long time after. The night was perfectly calm, and the air soft, and slightly scented with the new-made hay.

I had taken very little liquor, but enough to make me feel desirous of a few minutes' quiet rest. I thought of the old days when I used to come past this very spot every Sunday, carrying the biggest book I could get out of the Sunday-school library. I thought of all my struggles and ups and downs, and now how positions were reversed—my two cousins long since dead, my aunt still hale and hearty, but constantly worried about the future of her only grandson, a young man in the great city which I had just left.

Her son-in-law, for want of occupation, was fast sinking into the groove that her son had sunk into before he died. It was moonlight, but a yellow, soft moonlight, not bright, but diffused, and not marked with any sharp shadows. I could just see the outlines of the hills that shut in the valley.

I knew that my aunt's real Saturday night only began after ten o'clock, and the house was closed, so I walked very slowly till I reached the gate leading into the little field at the back of my aunt's house. Shaking off my reverie, I climbed over the gate and passed through the garden to my aunt's back-door, as, of course, the front one was locked. My aunt had a little supper ready, but her son-in-law had gone to bed. We talked in whispers, as a strange voice after hours might lead to inquiries.

My aunt was full of questions, but said very little of her own affairs; this, of course, I was prepared for. Care, not time, was beginning at last to tell on that iron frame; for herself she had no thought; she had plenty to keep her, but she wanted to keep all she had intact till her grandson was fairly settled in life. I knew the whole situation, but neither wished to sit as a dull, unsympathetic listener, nor yet intrude any advice, for this would have been fiercely resented. My own idea was that the son-in-law should be in the town looking after the welfare of his only son, but I might mount my bicycle and depart if I once dared to hint such a thing.

What I did say was that now, when I could run through on my machine any week-end, I would keep in touch with her, and if at any time I could advise her, or be of any service, she had only to drop a line and I would come. I went to bed, and the next morning strolled round the village. My aunt was always a late riser on the

Sunday, and the forenoon soon passed away. I had a little conversation with Mr. ——, her son-in-law, but he was already beginning to fail, both in his eyesight and hearing. I stayed with my aunt till three in the afternoon, which I thought was late enough, and then set off home.

Shortly after this I left my old employer, with whom I had been for a long time (that is, for the trade). We had no dispute, but the trade was still very good, and a young man named L—— had started building for himself, and had asked my employer to lend him a hand for a few days, to get his cornice ready. I was lent, and I never went back, though once or twice I worked (for a short spell only) for my old employer. My new place was a very pleasant one, and I gave so much satisfaction that when the firm for whom my son worked stopped building, my new employer gave my son a job at about twice the wages he had been receiving.

It was some days before I could shake off a feeling of melancholy whenever I thought of Mosston, but nothing that I could do could better the situation. I visited my aunt often, and hired a machine for a week-end, and took my eldest son with me. As he had not seen so much of the hill country as I had, we returned by a different route from the ordinary one, to enable him to see some real wild hill scenery.

But I got a lesson; a thunder-shower came on, and after the shower was over, and the sun came out again, the flies were so annoying that he nearly went mad. This was another of those country plagues that are never mentioned by those who rave about the country air and all that. I found them troublesome enough myself, but I set myself to bear them; but at one place I thought he was going to give in and lie down by the roadside.

As neither of us smoked (at least, at that time), we had to bear with them till we left the hills, when we had some relief. My youngest son, who was inclined to be delicate, stayed at Mosston with my aunt for about six weeks during the height of the summer. As my wife was very anxious about him, I said that I would get up soon on the Sunday morning, and run through in the cool air, and see how he was going on, and return home in the afternoon. The machine I had would be laughed at now as a mountain of iron, but I could not afford to buy one of the new pneumatics. I set off early, and landed at Mosston about eight o'clock.

After breakfast I went round among the two or three "old villagers," and the conversation fell upon cycling. It was agreed that it would make the country people independent of the trains, as they could go at any time, whereas the trains were few and far between. Aunt Kate's grandson had married, and was now engaged with the great problem of life. His father's eyesight and hearing were failing more than ever, and he was sinking into a lethargic state. My aunt complained of pains in her feet, but still did all the work herself.

Firm as a rock, she had chalked out her path, and nothing would turn her from it. Though pleased to see me at any time, and taking the greatest interest in the welfare of my family, I did not dare to make the only suggestion that I really thought would be for the benefit of all.

Perhaps it was because I never attempted to advise that my aunt actually unbent so far in her talks to me that it turned out, in the course of conversation, that her son, when he found himself going, had proposed the very thing which I would have proposed, and which was, as far as I could see, the very best thing to have done at the time.

But if her only son could not persuade her when he was passing away, it was not for me to propose it now, when it was, perhaps, too late. Nor did I attempt to ask her why she had not taken his advice. This was to give up the public-house, and go and take a house in the town. She had plenty of money to keep a household, even if she lived fifty years. Her son-in-law's and her grandson's future lay in the town, and she would be there to look after them, just as she was (at the time of our talk) looking after her son-in-law.

It was evident to me that my aunt was resolved to die in the house which had been her home during her long widowhood. Sixty-four years (as near as I can calculate) she had been a widow when the end came. She had seen her only son and daughter borne from this house to their resting-place in the hills, and nothing could induce her to leave it. I found out that the neighbouring people had proposed to present her with a testimonial, when she had been fifty years in it, but my aunt had resolutely declined it. There was nothing to do but let things go on. I came back to the town, and went about my own business.

For a time I had plenty to think about. The young man in whose employ I was took a contract, and, although he did not absolutely fail, yet lost sufficiently to prevent him from building any more for himself. This caused both my son and myself to find fresh berths. My youngest son had now finally left school, and, strangely enough, he was offered, and accepted, a situation immediately. His duties required him to work rather long hours, but it was not heavy work, and he was quite satisfied.

Thus far I had enjoyed pretty nearly thirty years' unbroken health, but a rather worrying job had left me run down, and my wife and I went for a week's holiday in the South of England. My employer congratulated me, on coming back, on the improvement in my health.

It was toward the end of the autumn, for I had waited for the completion of the job before going. My wife was delighted with the scenery and climate of the South, and, after an enjoyable week, I was busy for about three weeks, and looking forward to the turn of the year, when I intended taking another run out to Mosston.

The job on which I was working was situated in a part of the town about three and a half miles from where I lived.

One Friday evening, on coming home, there was a letter for me from Mosston. My aunt had fallen on the stone flags of the kitchen and injured herself. At her age (eighty-three) the worst might happen. I told my employer, and set out on the Saturday afternoon. I have spoken before of the awkwardness of the few trains, and it was too late in the season for cycling. I could only get the last train, and it was already dark when I reached the end of the railway.

I had a long and dreary walk up the hills before me, but my thoughts were such that the distance was never felt. Part of the road lay between plantations, and here I had to walk very slowly, as it was pitch-dark. I never met anyone till I was close to the village. I found my aunt in bed, and her grandson's wife and two great-grandchildren beside her.

My aunt had been going about her usual occupations in the morning, when something, she knew not what—perhaps dizziness—had caused her to fall. There was no immediate danger, though she never rose again from her bed. The same to the end, she wanted to know all the news and particulars of my late trip. I stayed over the Sunday, and returned on the Monday. There was a slight snowstorm, but the weather was clearing up, and I left with the understanding that if any grave symptoms should appear I would come at once. She lingered till about the beginning of spring, when she passed away in her sleep. By a strange combination of circumstances I was not at the interment. We did not live in the postal radius of the town, and a terrific drifting snowstorm which broke over the district rendered it impossible to cycle, or I would have set out straight for the burial-place by a route which would have missed Mosston altogether. The postal delivery left me no time to make arrangements for special conveyances—not an ordinary job for a workman. I had to bow to the inevitable.

One month after my aunt was laid at rest her son-in-law was laid in the same churchyard. The grandson's wife returned to her husband in the city, and the old house was closed, and finally pulled down.

CHAPTER XXVIII

I REMOVE TO THE CITY—CONCLUSION

ABOUT six months after this we again removed; we had been fourteen years and a half at the same place. We had seen our boys grow up there, and had passed many happy years; it was now 1898; the century was nearing its end. Both my sons wished to be nearer the city. I had always liked the suburbs, but it was quite right their wishes should be considered.

Time now seemed to fly past; my eldest son went to work in London for some time, and after he came back he married. Whilst never neglecting his handicraft, he has followed my advice and cultivated intellectual pursuits as a relaxation. An accomplished pianist, when I listen to his renderings of some of the standard overtures, I am doubly proud to think that the same hands can and do handle the tools of his trade. Classes for working men in mathematics and other sciences have for a long time been a great feature in this district, and he has quite recently passed at the head of his class, gaining the first prize.

My youngest son's lines have fallen in rather different places. More delicate in health than the eldest, his work is more of a mental than manual nature. Employed later in the evenings than the average working man, I have never asked him to join any of those classes which create such a healthful rivalry amongst young men, and have left him to improve himself in his own manner, no matter how desultory, confining myself to giving advice when asked.

But all has not been plane-sailing even in these late years. His health broke down once totally, and, after having been nursed with unremitting care by his mother for a long, dreary time, the doctor's order was that he must be taken at once to the South of England.

I now reaped the benefit of that week that I had spent there with my wife. She knew the place to go to and the route. She accordingly took him up herself, so that I could attend to my work.

A former curate of our parish was stationed not far from her destination, and he came to see our son, who had been in his choir. The local curate also took a kindly interest in the sick lad, and when my wife came away she had the satisfaction of knowing that he was amongst friends.

I have said that I never interfered with his methods of study, and the result was that he played the harmonium from the tonic sol-fa, which is Greek to me. The local curate had a harmonium at his lodgings, and expressed his surprise when my son said that he could play the Hymns Ancient and Modern from the sol-fa, but not from the old notation

As my son thought, by the tone of his voice, that he rather doubted it, I at once sent his music up to him, and he had the pleasure of playing all the familiar hymns and chants. The curate is now in a distant part of the British Empire, but my son receives letters from him from time to time. About four months in the South set my son on his legs again. On his return he was offered his old job, but I thanked them, saying I thought he could not stand it.

However, a different post fell vacant under the same employers, and my son obtained it.

I now come to the last and greatest change in my work and working life. Up to the end of the nineteenth century stone-cutting had always been comparatively free from machinery, I mean compared with other trades—joinery to wit. Saws I have seen from my boyhood, yet they were mostly employed on marble. But though I had often heard of these stone-planing machines, I had never seen them really ousting hand labour in this district till the dawn of this century.

I have heard that in Scotland there is already a reaction setting in against them ; that architects object that for about a quarter of an inch they stun the stone, and that this quarter of an inch soon peels off. This may be true or not, but they have almost revolutionized the trade already. On some jobs they run day and night.

Everywhere is heard the same wail from the workers, that they have destroyed the trade. I had been so well employed for a long time that

I had almost forgotten the treacherous smiles of fickle Fortune. I had finished up on one job, and gone on to another till about six years ago, when I found myself once more in the old predicament, seeking work in vain.

But this time I determined to go into the country. The machines are not so common there; but, on the other hand, the money is smaller, and there are both lodgings and house-rent to pay in the case of a married man.

I stumbled on a foreman who had charge of a job in the country. I had worked under him years ago, and on asking him for a job he said: "Yes, when the weather opens" (for a snowstorm had driven him into the town). I went, and had a chance of comparing the pros and cons of country *versus* town from the standpoint of a workman.

As usual, almost all the mechanics were brought from the town, for apart from the shopkeeper, and the publican and schoolmaster, nearly everyone was in the employ of the local squire.

The men from the town complained bitterly of the rates charged for board, and certainly, if what some of them said was true, they had reason to complain. However, I found good lodgings at reasonable rates. For a few weeks I stayed over the week-end at the village, only coming home once a month.

During these weeks I was struck with the unanimous cursing (yes, that is the word) of the dull Sundays by the men, and what follows shows that it was meant and not affected.

The railway companies were feeling the competition of the electric trams in the urban districts, and were starting week-end tickets, which were very popular.

All the mechanics at once availed themselves of them to return home every week, although there was a long walk to the station, and the ticket money—added to the board for five days and a half—cost more than staying in the village. In my case it was fifteen shillings and sixpence instead of fourteen shillings.

If we took a walk in the evenings, as a rule we were worried with flies, and when the summer came, we were annoyed with them during the day. Some of the men had to use paraffin to keep them off. In conversation with the people with whom I lodged, the question of "back to the land" cropped up. They assured me that all those people who went into the towns said that they could never stand the country again. While I was there one of the village young men came home from the South African War, and the whole place was in a ferment. The walking craze had reached the village, and most of the adult population were in training for a contest with another village.

One thing struck me—my landlord said that nine people had been taken away to the lunatic asylum in about twelve years. I hazarded a remark to the effect that I really thought the abolition of the old country excitements—bull-baiting, cock-fighting, pigeon-shooting, and wrestling—was to blame. When we went out to the village after the snowstorm, the nights were dark, and the total absence of lamps made it so that we dared hardly step outside, for there were some curious arrangements of stone steps and breakneck places, all well known to the villagers.

However, progress was to be seen. We were all paid by telegraph, and the village was in communication with the city. We finished the job by August, and then came to a rather celebrated old village nearer the city. There I spent the whole of the most beautiful autumn.

This village (at least, the old part) consisted of one fine old street set out in a graceful curve, with the houses at all angles; there was a wide stretch of green on both sides of the road, and a very plain old market-cross. Some of the old houses were a study for the artist. They had high roofs in two pitches, the bottom part covered with thin stone slabs and the top part bright red tiles. The windows were low, and glazed with small panes. Some of these houses had gardens both back and front.

In contrast to these, the new houses were utterly hideous in their dull uniformity. I lodged with a man who had got his shoulder injured and was taking lodgers to help him over the difficulty. He had been under the doctor about four weeks, and did not seem to be any better. One Saturday afternoon I left for home, and my landlord was going to see a bone-setter at a small town a few miles off.

When I came back on Monday I said: "How's your arm?" He immediately jerked it right up, and said: "It's all right now." As he was going up the main street of the small town in question, a young miner who was walking behind him hailed him: "Hi! do you know your shoulder is out?" He turned round, and the young man said: "It is out, and I will put it in for you in a minute. Stretch out your arm." The miner grasped his outstretched hand, and pressed on the shoulder with his left hand, and gave a sharp pull. "It is not in yet. That's because you are not in a house, and have your coat on. I'll put it in next try." He did, and my landlord went to work soon after.

We were putting double bay-windows and building a billiard-room on to one of the old houses for a works manager. When this was finished, I came back to my old haunts, and have never left them since.

A few years have rolled past since then. I have been fairly well employed, considering, as we say. Nothing has occurred to cause a ripple on the stream of life during those years, and these passages from my life are up to date.

It is to-day Easter, 1908, and I am writing these lines while my two sons are enjoying themselves in the next room.

My eldest has brought word that my two grandsons are busy spinning one of those new patent tops, with coloured paper discs, that their uncle has presented them with.

My wife, having satisfied herself that her grandsons enjoyed their Easter eggs, is busy preparing supper.

I linger over these last lines till a majestic melody comes from the other room. 'Tis the opening theme of the overture to Tannhäuser; one is at the piano, the other has taken the 'cello. One piece succeeds another till my wife opens the door: "Come, it is time to stop." Yes, it is time to stop.

THE END

BILLING AND SONS, LTD., PRINTERS, GUILDFORD

www.ingramcontent.com/pod-product-compliance
Lightning Source LLC
Chambersburg PA
CBHW080513090426

42734CB00015B/3036